THE CATHOLIC CHURCH AND THE FAMINE

In honour of all those
who work to relieve hunger and distress
among their fellow human beings

Donal A. Kerr

The Catholic Church
and the Famine

the columba press

First published in 1996 by
the columba press
55A Spruce Avenue, Stillorgan Industrial Park,
Blackrock, Co Dublin

Cover by Bill Bolger
Origination by The Columba Press
Printed in Ireland by Colour Books, Dublin

ISBN 1 85607 175 8

Acknowledgements

I am grateful to Ursula and Marcella Ní Dhálaigh, the late
Professor Tom O'Neill, Monsignor James O'Brien, David
Sheehy, Pádraig Ó Laighin, Larry Duffy, Brother Tom Connolly,
Kevin Duffy and Brian Keenan for their help and encouragement; to Marianna O'Gallagher for allowing me to consult
her invaluable work on Grosse Île while it was still at proof
stage; to Monsignor John Fleming and Father Liam Bergin for
access to the archive of the Irish College, Rome.

Contents

Introduction

'No imagination can conceive, no pen can describe it,' wrote Bishop Francis Haly from Carlow in January 1847. 'To have anything approaching a correct idea of the suffering of the poor, you should be here on the spot and see them with your own eyes!' These words are from one of many letters of priests who experienced the Great Irish Famine. The vivid nature of the correspondence of these men, eye-witnesses of the tragedy, brings home how horrific an experience it was. After a lapse of 150 years, it is the letters from those priests who were on the spot, saw with their own eyes and struggled to express the inexpressible, that provide the most poignant image of the catastrophe. By an extensive use of their own words – often in quaint, colourful English – this volume endeavours to convey some of that experience.

The volume is also an attempt to tell the largely untold story of the Catholic Church's response to the Famine, a response that was not confined to Ireland but came from every corner of the world. It is a story of generosity and goodness that brings the light of human compassion into the darkness of suffering and death which marked those years. From late 1847 on, however, assassination and eviction, rebellion and recrimination, brought to the surface contrasting attitudes towards the distress. At the national Synod of Thurles in 1850, the assembled bishops took a stand on the treatment of the poor which differed sharply from the attitude prevailing in much of public opinion.

This volume is not a history of Famine relief, much less a history of the Famine itself, but a description of how the Catholic clergy, especially, experienced that calamity and how it reacted. For this reason, it has not been possible to say much about the relief work of many charitable bodies and individuals such as the British Association, the Society of Friends and the Protestant Churches; the efforts of landlords who spent themselves for their people; the work of devoted doctors, nurses and officials. On the 150th anniversary of 'Black '47', this comparatively short volume may, however, serve to place on record the work of some of the many who did so much to help the victims of the Great Irish Famine.

CHAPTER 1

Experiences of the Famine 1845-7

The old priest Peter Gilligan
Was weary night and day;
For half his flock were in their beds,
Or under green sods lay ...
I have no rest nor joy nor peace
For people die and die.

W.B. Yeats

Although the main outlines of the Great Irish Famine, that greatest calamity of nineteenth century Europe, are well known, a brief sketch may be of use. In the winter of 1845, a blight came on the potato throughout Europe. In Ireland, where for 3 million of the population of 8.5 million the potato was the staple food, its failure could cause a major catastrophe. In 1845, the catastrophe did not come, because the failure rate of the potato in Ireland was 40% or less, the crop was an excellent one and Sir Robert Peel, Prime Minister of the United Kingdom of Great Britain and Ireland, promptly imported maize from America and sold it at 1d a pound. In 1846, however, from 75% to 90% of the crop failed, there was no bumper harvest and the new Liberal government of Lord John Russell (grandfather of Bertrand, the philosopher and anti-nuclear protester), decided not to import grain from abroad nor to interfere with market forces. As a result, in the winter 1846-7 people died in thousands. In the autumn of 1847, there was very little blight but the crop was small. In 1848, the crop failed disastrously again. This time the government decided that 'Irish property' (the landlords) must support 'Irish poverty'; since landlords, too, were impoverished, this meant more evictions, deaths, and emigration. The famine was not over until 1851.

Expectation and Disillusion

In the first year of the Famine, the clergy in the Dublin diocese provided some of the most important information on the
state of the country. The situation was serious in the prosper-
ous east coast area. Father John Smyth, parish priest of
Balbriggan, reported that 'there is not ... more than a fourth
of the crop safe from disease' and asked, 'what then is to become of them (the poor) or where will they get the money to
buy meal for their famishing families? Their only resource
will be the poorhouses and oh, what a blessing that we have
even that to fall back on'. The 'Poor Law' of 1838 had divided
the country into 130 administrative units or 'Poor Law
Unions', each of which levied a rate on local property to provide for the poor of the 'Union', including the establishment of
a workhouse or 'poorhouse' as it was often called. The regime
imposed in the workhouse was so harsh and degrading that
few would regard it as a blessing but, as Smyth foresaw, its role
became a central one during the Famine. The disaster Smyth
feared, however, did not come until a year later. When the
crop failed totally in 1846 the alarm of the clergy was tem-
pered by their confidence in government action. Fr Theobald
Mathew, the 'apostle of temperance', immediately contacted
Charles Trevelyan, the hard-working assistant-secretary to
the Treasury and the official in control of relief work, to tell
him that the potato crop was no more than 'one wide waste of
putrefying vegetation' and that 'the wretched people were
wringing their hands and wailing bitterly at being left food-
less'. Archbishop Michael Slattery of Cashel implored of
Lord Bessborough, viceroy from 1846 to 1847, to speed up relief. 'For heaven's sake let the public works begin,' he appealed. Archbishop John MacHale of Tuam wrote to the new
prime minister, Lord John Russell, that he had now a great
destiny to fulfil – 'the rescuing of an entire people from the
jaws of famine'. When he saw the 'afflicting appearance of
the potato fields' in Leinster, Archbishop Daniel Murray of
Dublin wrote in dismay: 'I do not know how the poor will get

through the winter.' Comparing the recurring Famine to the biblical seven-year famine in Egypt, when Joseph fed the whole country, he added: 'Hitherto, Sir Robert (Peel) has been our Joseph,' clearly hoping Russell, the new Prime Minister, would prove a new Joseph. In the recent past, the Liberals had shown themselves to be better-disposed to Ireland than the Conservatives and the Irish leaders, like Daniel O'Connell, expected much from the new Liberal Prime Minister, Lord John Russell. Russell had made 'Justice for Ireland' the central plank in his political programme and had dreams of bringing 'a golden age' to the country. Explicitly, too, at the onset of the Famine, he had publicly declared: 'I consider the Union [between Britain and Ireland] was but a parchment and an unsubstantial union, if Ireland is not to be treated in the hour of difficulty and distress, as an integral part of the United Kingdom.' It is not surprising then that the Catholic leaders, from Daniel O'Connell to the parish priests, confidently turned to him to handle the distress. Partly because of this confidence and also because they saw their role as promoters of peace, the clergy counselled calm and did all in their power to keep the people from violence.

By autumn 1846, when frightful accounts of impending starvation poured in from all over Ireland, the clergy, while imploring the government to act, counselled calm and trust in the authorities. At the outset of the Famine, the fishermen at the Claddagh threatened to sink the boats carrying grain out of Galway, but the prior of the Dominicans, Fr Nolan, persuaded them to abandon their plan. When, in August 1846, 10,000 Mayo peasants marched into Castlebar to protest that 'there is not a stone of sound potatoes among the whole of us', the curate, Father James M'Manus, told them that 'the Ministers of the Crown' were 'a humane and good government'. He reminded the people 'that Lord John Russell, than whom no better man lived, had declared "that no person in Ireland should die while England had the means to prevent it".'

Thomas O'Carroll, the curate in Clonoulty, County Tipperary, recorded, in his diary for September 1846, how he and his parish priest took action to prevent trouble in their parish:

> I tore down an inflammatory notice posted on the chapel gate, calling on the people to assemble on the Fair Green ... to devise some means to keep themselves from starvation. My attention was directed to it by Constable C. who ... told me he was afraid to pull it down.

In September, too, Father Terence O'Kane of Claregalway, County Galway, warning Bessborough, the viceroy, that the multitude were starving and that there was danger of popular outbreaks, appealed to him on behalf of the starving multitude 'confident that the prayer of the humble may be heard and his sorrows comforted'. A month later at Carrigtohill, County Cork, when a notice calling a meeting to demand that public work pay be raised to one shilling and sixpence a day was posted on the chapel doors, 'the clergy from the altars ... adjured their flock not to attend, and the meeting failed'. In Coolock, a few miles from the centre of Dublin, labourers met to complain of want of food and, while the curate spoke in favour of a society for the protection of the labouring classes, he used his influence to persuade them 'to separate peacefully and pay the strictest obedience to the law'. From County Clare, one of the worst hit areas, Captain Kennedy, the Poor Law inspector, reported that, with one exception, the priests 'seek to mitigate suffering and support the law'. Archbishop Murray invited the suffering to 'Look upon Jesus ... who having joy before him, endured the cross', reminding them that 'the sufferings of the present time bear no proportion to the glory to come'. The clergy believed they were being faithful to the role of 'ministers of peace' and following the line laid down by their trusted political guides, Daniel O'Connell and his son, John, who still trusted in the government.

The winter of 1846 was early and bitter but relief was slow in coming. 'I deem it a bounden duty,' wrote Father William

Flannelly of Clifden, 'to inform the government ... of the present misery of this parish. Some ... have left the last article of their nightly covering in the pawn office, and now lie at night on the cold bare earth, covered perhaps with some rotten straw or a handful of green wet grass.' Others had to sell their clothing and as a result 'cannot now appear at Divine worship ... or seek a day's work, on account of their nakedness'. From Swinford, County Mayo, Father Bernard Durcan complained that seven-eighths of the people would starve unless relief arrived. Desperately anxious to prevent violence, many clergy now found their efforts unavailing.

The sight of cart-loads of food bound for England, largely to pay the rents, particularly when funeral carts with Famine victims passed on the same road, sometimes led to riots, and army escorts were needed to protect the convoys of corn. In Croom, County Limerick, people stopped three loads of corn and it was only through the entreaties of the local curate, James Enright, that they let them pass. At O'Briensbridge, County Clare, on 8 October, a boat laden with corn was forced to turn back, despite its police escort; only the arrival of Daniel Vaughan, parish priest of Killaloe, prevented the mill being burned down. In the same month, an immense crowd of starving, angry people, marched into Macroom and gathered outside the workhouse demanding work and food. Their wives and children were 12 or 13 miles away, they said, and could not come to the workhouse and what was to become of them? Despite the presence of soldiers and armed police, a riot was prevented only by the intervention of the parish priest, Thomas Lee. Early in December, five or six thousand starving people marched into Listowel shouting 'Bread or Blood'! Despite the pleas of the parish priest, Jeremiah Mahoney, they refused to disperse. Exhausted from his exertions, Mahoney collapsed in a faint and, at this the local people protested that they (the demonstrators) might kill the priest, and the starving peasants dispersed. Bishop Kennedy of Killaloe made the proposal that the only way of preventing starvation was 'by the gentlemen of the country associating themselves for purchasing up the grain, which was at present being exported in such large quantities out of the country.' Nothing came of this generous suggestion. Even if all the food exported had been retained it would not have made up the loss of the potato crop, but it would have tided the people over the fatal gap before the arrival of grain from America in the Spring of 1847.

The false security induced by the previous year's successful relief work meant that the clergy, in common with most responsible citizens, believed that it was sufficient to alert the authorities who would take the necessary measures. Scores of priests wrote to the Dublin government explaining the situation and appealing for help. Meetings at which clergy of all denominations were represented met to voice public alarm at the growing disaster. Delegations, which normally included the local priest, travelled to Dublin or crossed to London to put the case of the starving to the viceroy or the prime minister.

Hopes Dashed

How the government would react became clear from the reception Sir Randolph Routh accorded to a delegation from Achill. Routh was the Dublin-based 'commissary-general for relief' that is, the army officer responsible for the provision of food. The delegation explained to him that because the merchants charged high prices, the people could not buy the corn and they asked him to sell food at a lower price. His reply was that 'it was essential to the success of commerce that the mercantile interest should not be interfered with'. Astounded, Father Monahan, the leader of the delegation, reminded him that in the previous year the government had sold at a cheaper rate in order to keep down the market price. Routh agreed but regretted it as a bad decision, for it gave bad habits to the people; the government, he affirmed, was now determined not to interfere with the merchants, but to act in accordance with the enlightened principles of political economy. Monahan said he could not understand why, at such a crisis as this, the government should be fettered by notions of political economy; political economy might be very well in its way, but the people of Achill knew nothing about it. Routh replied that there was nothing more essential to the welfare of a country than a strict adherence to the principles of free trade and begged to assure the reverend gentleman, that, had he read carefully and studied Edmund Burke, his illustrious countryman, he would agree with him that it was essential to the success of any measure of relief that the strict rules of political economy should be steadily attended to. Routh was referring to a pamphlet Burke wrote on *Thoughts ... on Scarcity* in 1795 and was insinuating that that most 'illustrious' Irishman would now oppose any interference with free trade. Monahan's astonished reply put his finger on a central issue of the Famine – how could a government insist on enforcing the principles of 'political economy', or free trade, if it meant starving its people? 'Political economy', in one form or other, was the prevailing economic theory in Britain; in Ireland it had an enthusiastic exponent in Richard Whately, Anglican Archbishop of Dublin. Economic development rather than relief work was its priority.

Routh was interpreting government policy correctly, for Russell gave the same message to those who travelled to London to intercede with him. The government was not prepared to interfere with 'market forces' and British public opinion felt Ireland should stand on its own feet and not depend on the government. To those who saw people wasting away with hunger, and who had confidently pinned their hope on the government, rigid attachment to these two principles brought incredulous dismay. Without government intervention and price control, the outlook was horrific, for the people could not purchase food. A clamour of protests arose. From Clifden, County Galway, Father William Flannelly, denouncing 'the slowness and the bungling of officials and the greed of the merchants and hucksters', complained that since the relief committees were forbidden to sell at less than market prices, they were clearly intended to protect the exorbitant famine prices charged by merchants. At a meeting held in the Music Hall in Lower Abbey Street, Dublin, the Reverend David Creighton, a Presbyterian minister, seconded a motion by Archbishop Murray, criticising the government 'who allowed the poor to perish sooner than interfere with the interests of the general trader'. The problem was not only the actual shortage of food but what modern historians call 'entitlement'; in other words, the poor had not the money, food-vouchers, etc to obtain food whose price had risen beyond their reach.

Experiences of the Calamity

The new year, 'Black '47', saw increased hardship. In the House of Commons, in February that year, the dying Daniel O'Connell, in his last speech to parliament, his voice now no more than a whisper, pleaded: 'Ireland is in your hands … if you do not save her, she cannot save herself.' Yet as no sub-stantial relief came, alarm increased. To Thomas Synnott, the very able relief worker whom Archbishop Murray employed to help him, John Madden, parish priest of Roscommon, dis-closed the growing desperation: 'We are doing what we can to distribute soup. What can we do? The applicants are so numer-ous, our means so limited.' Fr John Fitzpatrick's description of the appalling conditions in his parish of Skibbereen shocked readers in many countries, for his appeals were published in Irish, English, American and French papers. It brought jour-nalists to Skibbereen and as a result most of the illustrations of the Famine are from that district. The bishops were shaken by the distress. From Carrickmacross, in County Monaghan, Charles MacNally, Bishop of Clogher, gave a grim picture of what was becoming a daily scene:

> It would be impossible to give an idea of the deplorable state of our poor people. In this neighbourhood fever and

famine are making frightful ravages among them ...
Fourteen deaths in this parish on yesterday were reported
to me last night. It is wonderful how the clergy can bear
their unceasing labours attending on the sick and dying.

A sense of hopelessness in the face of so great a calamity is
evident in the letters of Dr French, Bishop of Kilmacduagh,
who wrote that 'we are so overpowered with the distress of
the multitudes. May God relieve them – the clergy and bishops
of Ireland never experienced such times!'

From Thurles, Archbishop Slattery described the situation in
the heartland of Munster:

> The distress of the people is every day increasing and per-
> sons, who three months ago were able to do without assist-
> ance, are now run out and are seeking relief. For some
> weeks past the deaths in this parish alone average from 15
> to 20 every week exclusive of the Poor House where on
> some days there have been 10 and 12 dead together ... It is
> undeniable that those public works are objectionable and
> tended ... to demoralise our people, but at the same time
> they were the means of keeping them alive, although they
> barely did the same.

When his oldest friend, Bishop Murphy of Cork, died,
Slattery predicted that his own time would soon come, for his
soul was 'sorrowful unto death and I think those happy who
are released from the calamities that have befallen our unhappy country'. Overcome by what he experienced, he
prayed: 'Oh, that I ... could fly from this wretched country into
some solitude where I might ... die in peace.'

In the privacy of his diary, that tireless relief organiser,
Archdeacon John O'Sullivan, parish priest of Kenmare, admitted the strain:

> I often think of betaking myself to some other country
> rather than see with my eyes and hear with my ears the
> melancholy spectacle and dismal wailing of the gaunt spectres

that persecute and crowd about me from morning until night imploring for some assistance.

This haunting by hungry faces and wailing voices pervades priests' letters to Archbishop Murray and to Paul Cullen, then rector of the Irish College in Rome, who acted as the Roman contact for many bishops and priests. Fr Coyne of Ballyhaunis wrote: 'If you could see my house surrounded every day with starving countenances, you would pity me.' Fr Madden of Roscommon related that his house was surrounded by the starving people 'calling for work or food'. Edmund French, Bishop of the dioceses Kilmacduagh and Kilfenora in Clare and Galway, told Cullen of 'the yellings of the poor, on the roads, in the streets ... at all our houses ...' The poor people did not know where to turn, as Eugene Coyne, parish priest of Ballyhaunis, reported:

> I encounter wherever I go the poor crying and saying that they have no person to tell them what steps they are to take in order to procure food or relieve them unless I do it, so may God relieve them.

It was not only the west and south that suffered. From Carlow, Bishop Haly, recounting that 'the deaths from starvation average more than fifty per diem' added that 'in one of the Dublin workhouses, it appears the deaths were fifty a week, so crowded were the unhappy inmates'. The priests had the role of making applications for relief. 'I am for hours every day employed in writing tickets for the dying applicants to the Vice Guardians and Relieving Officers, to give to the walking skeletons the food suited to their exhausted state,' wrote Peter Fitzmaurice, parish priest of Clifden. This role could spell trouble. Captain Douglas Labalmondiere, Poor Law Inspector for the Poor Law Unions (the 130 units into which the country was divided for the purpose of relief) of Tuam and Ballinrobe, denounced Father Hughes of Claremorris to the Parliamentary Committee on Poor Laws for taking too lenient a view of requests for food:

It was stated to me by the Reverend Mr Hughes, Roman Catholic clergyman for Claremorris, two days after I arrived in Ballinrobe Union, in the Boardroom, that he considered it to be 'morally justifiable to give certificates to get the starving creatures meal, without reference to the statements in them being correct'. I took down his words.

Although most of the priests worked flat out, writing begging letters and attending relief meetings and travelling on delegations to appeal for help, their duties limited the time they had available. The account of his daily life by Hugh Quigley, curate in Killaloe, merits citing at length:

We rise at four o'clock ... when not obliged to attend a night call ... and ... proceed on horseback a distance of from four to seven miles to hold stations of confession for the convenience of the poor country people, who ... flock in thousands ... to prepare themselves for the death they look to as inevitable. At these stations we have to remain up to five o'clock p.m. administering both consolation and instruction to the famishing thousands ... The confessions are often interrupted by calls to the dying, and generally, on our way home, we have to ... administer the last rites ... to one or more fever patients. Arrived at home, we have scarcely seated ourselves to a little dinner, when we are interrupted by groans and sobs of several persons at the door, crying out, 'I am starving', 'if you do not help me I must die', and 'I wish I was dead' etc. ... In truth the priest must either harden his heart against the cry of misery, or deprive himself of his usual nourishment to keep victims from falling at his door. After dinner – or, perhaps before it is half over – the priest is again surrounded by several persons, calling on him to come in haste – that their parents, or brothers, or wives, or children, are 'just departing'. The priest is again obliged to mount his jaded pony, and endeavour to keep pace with the peasant who trots before him as a guide, through glen and ravine, and over precipice, to his infected hut ... The curate has most commonly to say two Masses ... at different chapels; and ... to preach patience and resignation to the people, to endeavour to prevent them rising *en masse* and plundering and murdering their landlords. This gives but a faint idea of the life of a priest here, leaving scarcely any time for prayer or meditation.

Burying the Dead

As Famine-fever spread, a grim duty the priests now found thrust upon them was assuring that the dead received decent burial. People dreaded that they or their relations should be buried without a coffin and it often fell to the priest to procure coffins, to coffin the dead and to bury the victims of pestilence. 'My heart shudders,' reported Fr Peter Ward, a Connemara priest, 'when I hear the cry, "Here is a corpse", "Here is a corpse", "Here are three corpses devoured by wild beasts".' 'They are lying out in the fields,' Bishop McNally of Clogher, told Father Laurence Renehan, president of Maynooth College, 'and the people are so terrified that none but the clergy can be induced to approach. I yesterday sent a coffin out for a poor creature who died in a field, of fever, and have just heard that no one could be prevailed to put the body in it.'

Thanking Archbishop Murray for the £15 he sent, Martin Harte, parish priest of Doonfeny and Ballycastle, County Mayo, wrote: 'This day it was the cause of giving some consolation to a few individuals who had the remains of their friends unburied for four days for want of means to procure coffins.' From Kenmare, Archdeacon O'Sullivan recorded that there was 'nothing more usual than to find four or five bodies on the street every morning. They would remain so and in their homes unburied, had we not employed three men to go about and convey them to the graveyard ...' It was the same in Cork. Father Troy of Skibbereen recounted on 10 January

1847: 'I went to the hut ... provided with a coffin – had to creep in on my hands through an aperture. The lifeless and putrid corpse was reclining against the wall, and his wife and three spectres of children all but dead by his side. The poor woman and one of the children endeavoured to get to their knees (they could not stand) to help me to coffin his remains, but I had to beg of my curate to help us.' Joseph Kirwan, parish priest of Oughterard, and later first president of Queen's College, Galway, frequently coffined the dead himself. 'I had,' Thomas Quinn, parish priest of Inagh and Kilnamona in County Clare, told the Poor Law inspectors, 'together with my curate, Revd Mr Reid, to convey by torchlight two successive nights, the remains of two persons who were abandoned by their own immediate family and friends.'

Even the dreaded poorhouses, shunned now, not simply as degrading, but also as disease-ridden, became a refuge. 'Our poorhouse is crammed ... Still, thousands are craving admittance in vain, hoping to be coffined, rather than be exposed after death to dogs or wild birds of prey,' wrote another priest. They were often turned away from the door and Peter Ward, parish priest of Aughagower, County Mayo told Archbishop Murray of poor people 'banished from a crowded poorhouse, to die on the roads and (be) buried without coffins everywhere as the living are not able to carry their remains to the grave yard.' In Crookhaven, County Cork, the parish priest, Laurence O'Sullivan, reported that 'Of the hundreds that are borne to the graveyard not more than one half are enclosed in coffins; the remaining portion are wrapped in straw and borne upon a door – the bearers being the only funeral attendants.' Coffins could not be produced quickly enough or in sufficient numbers, and so, coffins with sliding panels or hinges were made; they were used again and again.

People died everywhere. Fr Denis Tighe of Ballaghderrin wrote to *The Tablet*, the English Catholic paper, that 'yesterday, a poor woman who went to chapel, her child, two years old, died in her arms from hunger in the house of God, during Divine Service'. In the end, even the holding of inquests, as required by law, had to be abandoned. Worse scenes were to follow. One of the Patrician brothers in Galway, John Lynch, brought a report to his horrified confrères, who were providing meals for children, of a woman who had been charged with murder for allegedly killing her child and eating part of it. James Maher, uncle of Paul Cullen and parish priest of Killeshan, County Carlow, wrote to tell of a poor woman who came home without any food for her children. One of them, maddened by hunger, bit off part of her arm.

Priests in Distress

The priests, who were mainly the sons of 'middling' farmers, were not dependent on the potato and did not suffer nearly as badly as the poor cottiers and labourers. A sharp fall in income and the rise in prices, however, caused hardship. Archdeacon O'Sullivan kept a careful account of the total income of his parish of Kenmare from 1840 which shows that from £348 in 1842 it plummeted to £116 in 1848. In the parish of Thurles the income dropped from £225 in 1844 to £177 in 1847. The well-informed Count Paul Strzelecki, the hardworking Polish-born agent for the British Association, the major relief organisation, told the viceroy in 1848 that the 'clergy are reduced to extreme want – even of common necessities' and a year later he reported that many of them were in 'a state of beggary' and without decent clothes. Later he told the parliamentary committee on Irish Poor Laws that 'In some instances, where priests were confined with fever, I found in their cabins nothing available beyond stirabout … there was no tea, no sugar, no provisions whatever; in some of their huts, the wind blew, the snow came in, and the rain dripped.' Other witnesses before the same committee, who also had been involved in poor relief, confirmed Count Strzelecki's reports. The following June, Thomas Redington,

the undersecretary to the government and a Galway landlord, reported that 'the priests have suffered severely, some
of them are almost starving'. Archbishop Murray related that
some priests were starving and others were unable to leave
their cabins or perform their duties for want of shoes.

Bishops were forced to refuse ordination to seminarians who
had completed their course, and came under mounting pressure to reduce the number of priests serving in the dioceses. 'I
am tortured by the applications of parish priests to remove
curates in consequence of the depopulation of their parishes,'
Bishop George Browne of Elphin exclaimed. Bishop James
Browne of Kilmore related that he had several well-qualified
priests just come from Maynooth, but he was obliged to quar-
ter them out amongst their relatives instead of employing
them in their ministry. 'And this,' he explained, 'not because
there was not the most crying need for their services', but because neither he (the bishop) nor his people had the means of
supporting them! The situation was worse in the diocese of
Kilmacduagh. 'My poor parish priests,' Bishop French
lamented, 'are obliged to dismiss their curates, owing to the
scanty means of subsistence for themselves!' Renehan, the
president of Maynooth College, pleaded with Bishop French
to ordain John Nestor who had completed his course. But the
bishop replied that if Maynooth could not keep him there
was only one solution – 'let him propose for the foreign mission or for America, as *I can't give him bread'*.

Most Famine victims died, not from starvation but from
Famine-related diseases to which relief workers, particularly
medical staff and priests, were constantly exposed. Catholics
demanded and expected the 'last rites'; indeed, for them this
sacrament had a priority over all the others and no one wanted
to die without the priest. Many priests, religious brothers and
nuns certainly died as a result of the Famine. By January 1847,
Bishop Egan of Kerry told Paul Cullen in Rome that he had
lost five priests by Famine fever. In June 1847, Father Denis

Murphy, writing from Kinsale, described 'the mortality
among priests' as 'beyond conception. We have buried 7 or 8
priests since the bishop's death' (the previous April). From
Cavan, Bishop Browne told Cullen in April: 'Two of our
priests in the bloom of youth have fallen victims of their zeal
and charity for the benefit of the poor. One of them was a stud-
ent of your College (the Irish College in Rome) ... Rev Dr P.
O'Reilly, a clergyman ... of the highest promise and could not
easily be excelled in talents, zeal, and usefulness.' Browne,
too, caught the fever but recovered; of the sixty-four priests in
his diocese of Kilmore, seven died in 1846-7, though it cannot
be established how many of those died as a result of the
Famine. From neighbouring Longford, Bishop Higgins told
Cullen that 'very many of our best priests have fallen victim
to pestilence, caught in the faithful discharge of their sacred
duties.' In the diocese of Killaloe a further five died, one of
cholera and four of famine-related disease in 1847-8. In July
1847, *The Nation* listed 28 clergymen who fell victim to the
Famine, of whom nineteen were Catholic and nine
Protestant. On 14 August 1847 *The Nation* announced the
deaths from fever of three priests, of whom two, it was explicitly noted, had contracted the disease 'in the discharge of
their duty'. For 1847, the *Catholic Directory* listed eighteen
priests who died from fever for the month of May alone.
During 1847, over forty priests in Ireland fell victim to the
Famine. Others died in England. From Liverpool, a Christian
Brother reported, on 16 June 1847: 'The clergy here in
Liverpool are dropping still with typhus fever. Father
Graystone, successor to Father Parker, St Patrick's, died last
night ...' From Manchester, Brother John Norris related: 'It
was a melancholy thing to see two priests carried in the same
funeral to the grave. These were – Fathers Walmsley and
Metcalf, and only a fortnight previously two others – Fathers
Wilson and Carr; and a little after them Father Coppinger, the
best of all, the grandnephew of the great Doctor Coppinger,
Bishop of Cloyne.' In Bolton, Father John Dowdall, parish

priest of Saint Peter and Paul, died of typhus contracted 'in the discharge of his duty'. Three or four Christian Brothers also died. These losses were a severe blow to the church. Saint Patrick's Church, Liverpool, was forced to close down. 'What more alarming', wrote a Christian Brother in Manchester, 'than not to be able to find in the whole of the large city of Manchester for a time, a single priest to attend the dying.'

Effects of Black '47

The suffering during those few months of 'Black '47', as that winter was called, was horrifying. Bishop O'Higgins of Ardagh told Cullen: '711 died during last season in Gortleitra, one of our ordinary country parishes – Most of them were buried by night in bags, cabbage plots, and in the cabins where they departed.' From Killarney, Bishop Egan wrote: 'Whole families, nay whole villages (are) swept away.' The entry which Father Michael Lane made in the Baptismal Register for his parish of Donoughmore, County Cork, in March 1847, summed up the horror of that terrible winter:

> This was the Famine year; there died of the Famine from November 1846 to February 1847, over 1,400 of the people (almost a third of the population) and one priest, the Reverend Dan Horgan, *Requeiscant in Pace*. Numbers remained unburied for over a fortnight, many were buried in ditches near their houses, many without a coffin. Four men were employed to bury the dead and make graves and two, and sometimes four, carpenters to make coffins.

'May God relieve them', wrote Bishop French, 'the clergy and bishops of Ireland never experienced such times!' Though each priest's experience was limited to his own parish, the harrowing ordeals they all describe in their letters were so similar as to be practically identical. This terrible sameness brings into starker relief the horror they witnessed. Used as they were to scenes of misery, famine and fever in poverty-stricken Ireland, they had never experienced scenes like this. They saw and heard what they never believed could happen. The gruesome scenes they witnessed, the constant clamouring of people looking for bread, the hovels which the evicted erected over ditches, the unburied dead, the half-devoured corpses, 'made the heart shudder', as one of them said. Death was close to themselves, too, when they brought to the dying thousands the last rites of the church and they saw some of their fellow-priests die the horrid death of typhus. No wonder many wished to flee from it all. Archbishop Slattery revealed his depressed feelings to his friend and codiocesan, Laurence Renehan, president of Maynooth: 'Verily, we are fallen upon time that will try men's souls and prove what spirit they are of; oh, never did the Mission of Ireland require the humble, patient, hardworking and disinterested priesthood more than at present.' The psychological cost is difficult to measure, though other similar catastrophes may afford insight. As the disaster dragged on, Count Strzelecki suggested that some were shaken in their faith in God

The clergy's expectation that Russell and his government would prove another 'Joseph' and save the people from the second year of Famine had proved an illusion. Some, like Bishop Haly writing to Cullen in Rome, defended government efforts, explaining that 'if they [the government] have been only partially successful, we must recollect that it is a *nation* that suffers; it is a *nation* that cries for food.' The scale of the disaster was so great, he believed, that the government could not have coped. Others reacted like MacHale, who in as vitriolic a letter as ever proceeded from his sharp pen, warned Russell in terms worthy of the great prophets of the Old Testament: 'If you are ambitious of a monument, the bones of a people, slain with the sword of famine, piled into cairns more numerous than the ancient Pyramids, shall tell posterity the triumphs of your brief but disastrous administration.' Haly's view that the scale of the disaster was so great that government could not possibly have coped and MacHale's view that disastrous government policy led to the slaying of the Irish people, were both to find echoes in later assessments of the Famine.

Under pressure from the Irish administration, horrified by the number of deaths now running into hundreds of thousands, the government, in March 1847, began to set up soup-kitchens. Slow at first in getting started, before long soup-kitchens were opened up all over the country, and they saved countless lives in the late spring of 1847. By July, three million were being fed. It was the government's most successful reaction to the famine.

When the horrors of 'Black '47' became known, they evoked a generous response from many different quarters, including the Catholic Church.

CHAPTER 2

Relief Work

Since the Irish, with the English, Welsh and Scots, were equal subjects of Queen Victoria within the United Kingdom, responsibility for ensuring their relief from starvation rested with parliament and government in London. Voluntary relief societies also sprang up to help. The first relief aid came from India, where Irish and British residents, and, in particular, the Irish soldiers, sent £15,000 through the Calcutta Relief Committee. Then in September 1845, Lord Cloncurry set up the Mansion House Relief Committee in Dublin. This was followed, in December 1846, by the setting up of the General Central Relief Committee, which included Archbishop Murray, the Provost of Trinity College, the Dean of Saint Patrick's Cathedral, the Marquis of Kildare and the Lord Mayor of Dublin. As the Famine worsened, Stephen Spring Rice, Lionel de Rothschild and Thomas Baring (of Baring's bank) founded, in January 1847, the British Association for the Relief of Extreme Distress in Ireland and Scotland, which raised huge sums of money from the generosity of the wealthier classes in England. Religious groups, too, were to the fore in organising relief. The Society of Friends founded a Central Relief Committee and used its contacts in Britain and the United States to finance a very effective relief mission. Protestant and Catholic clergy threw themselves wholeheartedly into relief work. *The Freeman's Journal,* a nationalist daily newspaper, remarking on 'the perfect harmony which distinguishes the ministers of religion of all classes', commented:

The Catholic and Protestant clergymen vie with one another in acts of benevolence. They are the most active members of relief committees – they confer together, remonstrate together, evoke together the aid of a dilatory government, and condemn together its vicious and dilatory refusals.

Joseph Bewley, one of the joint secretaries of the Society of Friends Committee, assured the Select Committee on Irish Poor Laws that they 'found none more efficient than the Protestant Clergy: the means they possessed in the aid of their wives and daughters, of attending to the wants of the poor, rendered their services very valuable.' The Catholic clergy, too, Bewley told the Poor Law Committee, 'were ... exceedingly useful', pointing out, however, that they had not the advantage of the help of wives and daughters. Their duties in bringing the sacraments or last rites to the sick and dying left them with less time for ordinary relief work. Fr John Fitzpatrick reported from Skibbereen that although his two extra curates devoted their entire time to the sick and dying, they could scarcely afford them the last rites, while from Balla, County Mayo, the parish priest, Martin Browne, grieved that his curates were 'toil-worn in ministering to the starving poor'. When the curates, who outnumbered the parish priests and constituted the younger and more active section of the clergy, were excluded, at Trevelyan's behest, from the relief committees, Lord Monteagle protested to Lord Bessborough, the viceroy: 'You also exclude all the Roman Catholic curates. Without them, and here they are labouring like tigers for us working day and night, we could not move a stroke.'

The priests, although generally not wealthy, were able to do considerable relief work, for they were in receipt of substantial relief funds. Some of this money came from the British Association, the General Central Relief Committee and the Society of Friends. The Irish church, however, through its overseas network, managed to generate a substantial flow of relief money from all over the Catholic world. This largely unknown Catholic relief work kept thousands alive during the worst periods of the Famine.

At first some priests gave from their own monies, as for instance James Maher, uncle of Paul Cullen and parish priest of Killeshan, who sold his horse and gig to raise money. Soon, however, they had to appeal for outside help. Relief money came from individuals or groups who normally sent it directly to the area where the need was and, as a result, little record remains. From January 1847 on, much of it came to Archbishop Murray, who was among the first to organise widespread voluntary aid. Murray, over the many decades that he was archbishop, had gained a reputation for personal goodness, pastoral care and charitable activities. This stood the eighty-year-old bishop in good stead now; relief funds came to him from all over Europe, and as far away as America, Africa and Australia. Among the earliest recorded gifts he received for relief were ten guineas from two English Protestant lawyers in Lichfield. His extensive network of charitable and often well-to-do friends, came to his aid. In January 1847 Lady Lucy Foley, the widowed aunt of the Duke of Leinster, sent Murray £100 (approximately £8,000 in today's money) from Marseilles. Mary Leonora Sheil from London sent him a similar amount. Murray sent the monies directly to the priests and religious for distribution – a more expeditious and less wasteful manner than government relief. As Bishop O'Donnell of Galway pointed out, the advantage of dividing the relief monies among the parish priests was that they would know the most needy cases in their own parishes. Later, Murray brought in Thomas Synnott, who had experience in relief work, to deal with the correspondence and distribution of relief. Synnott's efficiency won him praise from many priests. Martin Browne, parish priest of Balla, told him that 'your untiring exertions have contributed under heaven to save the lives of thousands.'

In Kenmare, County Kerry, the enterprising Archdeacon

O'Sullivan, at his own risk, imported food which he sold at cost price and then used the money to import again and recommence the process and so managed to distribute cheaply £30,000 worth of food. He told a parliamentary committee: 'I felt that it was an unusual business for a person in my sphere of life to turn flour merchant, but still someone must have done it at the time.' Others, like Fr Daniel Vaughan in Killaloe, bought potatoes which they cut up for seed and distributed free.

Religious Orders

Despite their small numbers, the religious orders – priests, brothers and nuns – made an impressive contribution. Fr Mathew pleaded the cause of the Famine victims with Trevelyan at the Treasury in Whitehall and with Cardinal Acton in Rome, and used his many contacts in England and America to help him set up a soup-kitchen in his own house in Cork. The Dublin Carmelite, John Spratt, organised an interdenominational relief committee in Dublin where 'to perpetuate the kind feeling now so liberally evinced in favour of our starving people by those of every class and creed, in the distribution of relief there shall be no religious distinction whatever'. Convents everywhere provided meals and, in particular, breakfasts for the children. Sr Mary O'Donel of the Presentation Convent in Galway wrote that 'We are struggling to keep on our breakfasts as the only means (the children) have and to clothe the destitute orphan.' Among those convents that were active in providing relief were the Presentation Sisters in Galway, Tuam, and Doneraile, the Sisters of Mercy at Tuam, Westport, Birr and Charleville, the Ursuline Sisters in Elphin, the Sacred Heart Sisters in Roscrea, the Sisters of Charity in Oranmore, the Poor Clares in Newry and Loughrea, the Carmelite Nuns in Loughrea, the Dominican Sisters in Athenry, and the Dominican Friars at the Claddagh of Galway. In Galway, too, the Patrician Brothers, under the leadership of Paul J. O'Connor, set up an Orphans' Breakfast

and Clothing Institute which at one stage was giving breakfast to a thousand children, as well as feeding 400 to 500 poor
in their homes. The Annual Report for 1847 read: 'It is resolved that while a penny or particle of food remains in the
establishment, or can be obtained by the humblest entreaty,
not one of the little creatures will be cast overboard.' Two
years later, Brother Paul wrote to *The Tablet* to thank an
'English Protestant Lady ... who has not ceased from the beginning of the Famine to contribute to the relief of the poor of
Ireland'. Brother John Leonard, superior of the Christian
Brothers in Peacock Lane, in Cork city, told his confrères: 'We
must feed the children we have before taught, and to do this
let us first begin with ourselves and make some sacrifices for
their sakes.' Thanks to 'the charity of our friends in England',
they were able to give one meal a day to four hundred children. With the support of Quaker families, the brothers in
Sexton St, Limerick, had a cauldron of stirabout ready for the
children each day. The abbot of the Cistercian abbey of Mount
Melleray, County Waterford, described the situation there:

> Even in this isolated place, on a most ungrateful and profit-
> less mountain, we relieve from eighty to a hundred wand-
> ering poor daily, besides thirty-three families around us
> ranging from four to ten in each, who are our regular
> weekly pensioners and whom we have, under God, saved
> from hopeless starvation. To have been enabled to do even
> this little for the sons and daughters of God, is a luxury be-
> yond the banquet of kings.

Help from Britain

English Catholics organised relief. Of special note was the
work of Frederick Lucas, editor of *The Tablet*. Shocked by the
reports from Ireland, Lucas, a convert to Catholicism and to
Irish nationalism, complained that English Catholics were
not doing enough for the Famine victims and used *The Tablet*
to launch and sustain a significant fund-raising campaign.
Some, like Lord Shrewsbury, were generous; in January 1847

The Tablet reported that he gave £100 and that Lady Shrewsbury 'sends £50 to her native county, Wexford'. In every issue of *The Tablet* lists of contributions and letters of thanks from all over Ireland appeared. An anonymous Scottish priest wrote to the editor: 'I have only one pound in my pocket and I cannot refuse it to the dying Irish. I am sorry that my poor congregation cannot contribute a baubee.' In one issue of *The Tablet* £342 were raised, including articles of plate, a gold watch from a priest and £1.3s from '11 poor Irishmen'!

Another great organiser of relief in England was Bishop John Briggs, vicar-apostolic of the Northern district. He had visited Connacht and had a deep love for the people. He issued a pastoral to all his churches pleading for prayers and from January to Easter of 1847, had a weekly relief collection taken up. Briggs's episcopal colleagues, Thomas Griffiths, vicar-apostolic of the London District, Nicholas Wiseman, his successor, and Francis Mostyn, vicar-apostolic of the Northern district, were also generous. Two famous Italian missioners in England, the Rosminian, Luigi Gentili and the Passionist, Dominic Barberi, who received Newman into the Catholic Church in 1845, were active. Barberi raised £21 at Aston and Stone and his community added a further £4 by putting a small silver chalice up for sale, Barberi remarking that 'it was a maxim of the ancient Fathers and Doctors of the Catholic Church that, in case of the people being in extreme distress, it is lawful to sell the sacred vessels of the church to relieve the poor, who are the real vessels of election.'

Pope Pius IX, Rome and the Italian Church

Normally, the provision of relief was left to the government of the distressed country, but many foreign countries proved extraordinarily generous to famine-stricken Ireland. O'Connell's astonishing career had aroused a sympathetic interest in Ireland. This was particularly true of European countries with which Ireland had long-established links.

Bishop Gaston de Bonnechose of Carcassonne, in his appeal to his people for help for Ireland, told them that their alms would be offerings on the tomb of 'the great O'Connell, the hero of Christianity, the new Judas Maccabeus, who bravely defended the rights of a people for long wrongfully oppressed and who died gloriously for religion and liberty'. Important, too, was the zealous activity of Irish people in those countries. One of the earliest continental donations came from an Abbé Moriarty in Dieppe.

In Rome, the students and staff of the Irish College did without meals to raise money. In Rome, too, the Committee of British Residents set up an Irish Relief Committee which included John Pakenham, John Harford and also Paul Cullen and Tobias Kirby, rector and vice-rector of the Irish College. They received encouragement and financial support from the new and liberal-minded Pope, Pius IX. The leader of the Liberal Catholics, Padre Gioacchino Ventura, who had great influence with Pius IX, and was an ardent admirer of O'Connell, threw in his weight behind relief measures.

Paul Cullen was among the most active campaigners for Irish relief. He wrote to bishops all over Italy asking for help and was rewarded with many contributions. Cullen asked his sister to auction the cross she possessed, which apparently was a papal gift. He also wrote to his brother, Thomas, in Liverpool, appealing to him to give what he could and Thomas replied on 23 February 1847 that he had raised £600 and would send £400 more before the month was out. Liverpool Catholics, the Cullens recounted, raised £3,000 in relief. Cullen's nephew told him of the work of Fr Maher, Cullen's uncle, and then went on to relate: 'My uncle Patrick has a dinner party of from seventy to one hundred poor people every day in the week. Uncle Garret has given a suit of clothes to thirty or forty people beside a great deal of food to the poor.'

As early as January 1847, Pius IX, shocked by the Famine

news, sent 1,000 Roman dollars to the Irish bishops, and appealed to the Roman clergy and people to help. His example was followed by Cardinal Fransoni, secretary to the Congregation of Propaganda, and Cardinal Mai, the Prefect of the Congregation of the Index. At a triduum of prayer in Sant' Andrea della Valle, Ventura preached in Italian on the first day; on the second day, the Bishop of Montreal, where so many Famine refugees were arriving, preached in French; and, on the third day, Cullen preached in English. The Romans responded generously. Diamonds and gold rings and gold watches poured in. A priest gave the silver buckles from his shoes, probably the only thing he had to spare, as Cullen remarked. Two Italians made an unusual gift-offering – 2,000 cubic palms of marble!

On 25 March 1847, however, distressed at the continuing bad news, Pius took the unprecedented step of issuing an encyclical, *Praedecessores Nostros*, appealing to 'the Patriarchs, Primates, Archbishops and Bishops' of the whole Catholic world on behalf of the Famine victims. He asked them to appoint three days for public prayers and 'to exhort your people to give alms for the relief of the Irish people', reminding them that 'the beauty of wealth lies not in the manner of life of the rich but in food given to the poor'. His appeal made a powerful impact on the Catholic world. In Italy, many bishops had responded to Cullen's appeal, but now very many more sent funds. Among those who contributed were the Bishop of Rieti and Loreto who set aside the Lenten alms in his dioceses for the Irish. The bishops of Turin, Terni, Aoste, Genoa, Aqui, Aosta, Mondovi, Susa, Sarzana also sent relief. Bishop Morenzo of Ivrea, from his small and penurious diocese, sent two subscriptions, the second one of 4,000 francs, and recounted that a very lively devotion still existed in his diocese to Blessed Thaddeus McCarthy who had died there in 1492!

Other European Countries

Even before the pope's appeal was issued, French bishops and organisations were raising funds for relief. French sympathy had historical and religious roots and had taken deeper root over the previous twenty years because O'Connell's movements for Catholic Emancipation and Repeal had caught the imagination of Catholic Europe, particularly in France. In February 1847, French Catholics had requested the pope to issue a general appeal to bishops everywhere to make a combined effort for the famine-stricken Irish, a plea that may also have influenced Pius IX. In May, a committee, which included Baron de Schauenberg, the Comtes Montalembert and de Mérode, the Vicomtes de Falloux and d'Harcourt, was established to co-ordinate aid for the Irish, 'a people to which France is bound by so many memories', and they expressed the hope that the committee would include men of all political persuasions and social positions. Montalembert had first-hand knowledge of Irish famine – he had organised subscriptions through the Liberal Catholic paper, L'Avenir, for the victims of the distress in Connacht in 1831 and had maintained a lively interest in Irish affairs. The leading Catholic papers, the ultramontane L'Univers, the liberal Catholic Le Correspondant, and the moderately ultramontane L'Ami de la Religion, carried reports of the continuing disaster and frequent appeals for subscriptions.

When Pius IX launched his appeal, French bishops reprinted it, many of them commenting critically on England's failure to cope adequately with the Famine and on England's Irish policies in general. Cardinal de Bonald, Archbishop of Lyons, whose proud title was 'Primate of Gaul', in a passionate appeal for help for Ireland, wrote to his people:

> If unjust prejudices have prevented that unfortunate island (Ireland) from enjoying the liberty which would restore life to her; if ... that Catholic nation is kept in a humiliating state of minority by a sister-island, which prevents her

from enjoying her most legitimate rights, then let us at least console her heart by our most tender compassion ...

The bishops' appeals were successful. Already by July 1847 large sums had poured in; the diocese of Strasbourg headed the first list with 23,365 francs. Individual priests and laity also were moved to collect for the relief of the Famine-victims. By August 1847 the fortnightly review, Le Correspondant, reported that 'in the midst of the increasing and frightful misery in our countryside, the appeals made by our bishops have yielded more than 300,000 francs ...' Although the report was concerned solely with Ireland, some of the money may have been sent to the Lebanon. The Archbishop of Paris, Cardinal Affre, sent £750 direct to MacHale and the Bishop of Arras sent a further £247.7.6. One Frenchman wrote to Murray to tell him that his little daughter, when dying, implored him to send whatever dowry he intended for her, to the poor Irish. Another Frenchman, who described himself as a domestic servant, forwarded a sum which he had amassed by making economies in his expenditure (vue mes économies). The Society of St Vincent de Paul sent aid from many countries. The Irish branch, which included John O'Connell, the Liberator's son, and Charles Gavan Duffy, the Young Irelander, took on the task of distributing relief collected by the parent body in France. Its relief expenditure amounted to some 150,000 francs in 1847 alone. From Turkey, the Constantinople branch of the Society contributed £284. The Sultan himself, Abd-el-Medjid, moved by the horrific accounts his Irish doctor gave of the Famine, sent the sum of £1,000.

Belgian and Dutch Catholics also responded generously and the dioceses of Malines, Bruges, Ghent and Antwerp all sent considerable sums. O'Connell's campaigns had impressed many German states, particularly in the Rhineland and Bavaria, and the dioceses of Augsburg, Cologne, Munich, Trier, Aachen, Bonn, Münster, Paderborn, and Culm raised large sums. From the Austrian Empire, too, considerable amounts were sent to Murray for the 'relief of Irish Catholics'. From Tarragona in Spain, the editor of the *Revista Catolica* sent £43 and the Bishop of Cartagena 50 francs. Bishop Louis Pavy of Algeria issued a pastoral on Ireland which was touching in its emotion and well-informed in its facts on Ireland – 'the land of St Patrick, Columkill, Columbanus and Virgilius' (of Salzburg). Citing the words of Christ, 'come to me all you who suffer and I will bear you up', he begged of Algerian and African Christians to imitate the generosity of the great Saint Cyprian of Carthage to those in need.

The New World

Apart from these European countries, another source of relief had opened up in the new countries. From the neginning of the century, the Irish had emigrated in great numbers, and now from America, Australia, Canada, Newfoundland, South Africa, the West Indies, and India, Irish and English, Protestants and Catholics, sent relief. Irish soldiers serving abroad were openhanded in helping their fellow-Irishmen. In Gibraltar, the bishop, Henry Hughes, found the soldiers among the most generous in contributing, and from Bombay, Bishop Luigi Fortini told Murray that 'almost all the Irish Catholic soldiers and many other persons have made a collection for the starving Irish.' From Capetown and Port Elizabeth in South Africa, from Montevideo in Uruguay and Caracas in Venezuela, Irish priests strained to keep relief monies flowing to Ireland. From Buenos Aires, Anthony Fahy from Loughrea, County Galway, the Dominican chaplain to the Irish in Argentina, sent over £600 for relief. On behalf of the diocese of Caracas in Venezuela, Father Laurence O'Callaghan sent two sums amounting to £107. Away in the Indian Ocean, on the tiny island of Mauritius, the Black and Creole people were moved to tears by the account their pastor, Father Jacques-Désiré Laval, the 'apostle of Mauritius', gave of the suffering in Ireland and subscribed liberally.

Australia was very generous. At Port Philip, in Victoria, Fathers Patrick Geoghegan and John O'Shannassy set up an Irish Relief Fund which sent £500 to Ireland in August 1846 and a further £863 the following October. In New South Wales, a committee for the Relief of Distress in Ireland and Scotland was set up and its secretary, George King of Pitt Street, Sydney, was able to send £600 to the British Association for the relief of distress. Later he sent £400 to both archbishops of Dublin, Catholic and Anglican. Father Henry Gregory OSB, secretary to the Archbishop of Sydney, John Bede Polding, sent £118 to Murray and told him that £3,000 had been raised in other parts of New South Wales and would be sent on to the British Association. From Sydney, too, Father John McEncroe sent a further £118. Maria Jones of Bathhurst sent £40 for the Dublin victims and Brigid Canton of Mittagong £100 for the suffering in the Liberties in Meath Street, Dublin. Hobart, Tasmania, set up a relief committee that continued to send relief during 1846 and 1847.

North America

The American peoples were most generous. State governments, senators, mayors, bishops, priests, Choctaw Indians in Oklahoma, ex-slaves, American soldiers fighting in Mexico and Mexicans themselves all contributed. Perhaps the earliest to organise was Fr Thomas O'Flaherty, parish priest of Salem, Massachusetts who, in December 1845, set up an Irish Charitable Relief Fund and collected over $2,000. In July 1846 the Irish papers recorded large sums sent by Irish priests to bishops and priests in Ireland. In December 1846 the Society of Friends in New York began their well-organised relief work. They set about raising subscriptions 'from the rich … through John J. Palmer, President of the Merchants' Bank and (from) the poor through the R.C. Bishop Hughes'. Bishop Hughes maintained an active interest in the Famine, but other Irish-born bishops also played their part. In February, John Fitzpatrick, Bishop of Boston, read his pastoral on the Famine to his congregation and that night a relief committee was set up. By March, it had sent $20,000 to Archbishop Crolly, of Armagh. In all, the diocese of Boston subscribed $150,000. Bishops Peter Kenrick of Saint Louis, Michael Portier of Mobile and many others kept funds flowing to Ireland. Congress lent a warship, the *Jamestown*, on which food was so packed that the guns were removed to make room. Then, in the record time of fifteen days, Captain Robert Forbes of Boston and volunteer sailors, sailed it into Cork harbour to cheering crowds. The Quakers distributed the food through the Catholic clergy. Two months later, the *Macedonian*, captained by George De Kay from New York, repeated this act of mercy.

The relief organisers remarked that it was the Irish emigrants who were the most generous in contributing to their funds. Of perhaps even greater importance in keeping their relatives alive were the immense sums, running into millions of dollars, the Irish Americans sent in the eagerly-awaited 'American letter', in which was often enclosed a ticket to America.

Canada was also generous. From Halifax, the Irish-born William Walsh, Bishop of Nova Scotia, sent the sum of £125 in 1847. He told Cullen that at a meeting in Halifax he received £500 there and then and hoped to be able to send £3,000 more before long. At much the same time, Bishop Dollard of New Brunswick sent relief. In February 1847, the Archbishop of Quebec, Joseph Signay, had launched an appeal for help and funds poured in from all over French Canada, the little group of Irish at Lachine contributing £41. In Canada, too, a number of Indian tribes contributed to the relief fund.

Catholic relief continued right up to 1850 and the £10 (£800 in today's money) Murray continued to send to priests in the most distressed areas, kept many alive. It was all the more necessary then, because, at the end of 1847, Trevelyan decided that the distress was over. In 1849, the Society of Friends, after telling the government that the relief work was beyond the

reach of private exertion, wound down its heroic work.
Evictions

After the winter of 1847 the number of evictions soared,
mainly as a result of the Poor Relief Extension Act of 1847 and
its 'Gregory clause' which barred public relief to anyone
holding more than a quarter-acre of land. The number of
families evicted in 1846 had been 3,500; in 1847 it rose to 6,000
and in 1848 to 9,700. From County Mayo, Thomas Timblin,
parish priest of Ballisakeery, lamenting that 'hundreds of *my
poor parishioners must necessarily perish'*, revealed that besides
famine and fever, there was a new threat – death through exposure:

> they must as a *sine qua non* condition give up not only the
> possession of their small patches of land but also level
> their cabins, thereby leaving themselves no other shelter
> than that of gathering the former roofing of their cabins
> and placing them on the ditches, there to perish not by
> hunger alone but by cold.

Forcing unfortunate tenants to level their own cabins was
against the law. The condition of the evicted whose houses
were 'tumbled', that is, levelled, was vividly portrayed by
James Dwyer, parish priest of Lackagh, Claregalway:

> the parties (the evicted poor) are most hideously circum-
> stanced, such as dying on the road side or under the
> bridges or in sheds where a few sticks are erected for their
> reception, to be visited by myself who am doomed fre-
> quently to crawl on my knees into the abode of death.

Fr Thomas Brady, of Drung, near Cavan, complained that:

> In this parish ... there are fifty farms vacant, two hundred
> human beings sent adrift in an inclement weather to beg
> or die ... As I meet them on the highways, livid corpses
> raised from the grave, I can but give a faint idea of their
> wretched appearance ... wishing for the happy release of
> death ... The landlords exterminate right and left.

John McCullagh, parish priest of Spiddal, revealed that 'the priest is called on every other day to attend from two to five dying persons where more than fifty houses were tumbled down last winter, the persecuted starving outcasts living in ditches or in sheds.'

Fr Edward Waldron, Ballinrobe, chillingly described the result of some evictions just before Christmas:

> We had the last visit from the Sheriff here two days before *Christmas-day*, with horse and foot soldiers and a posse of men well paid ... for evicting the starving tenants and tumbling houses. These poor evicted people (forty-eight families) are wandering about at present as there was no room for them in the workhouse and if you were to see where some of them slept at night! I can only say that it was not fit for pigs. Man made to God's image and likeness to be thus treated by fellow man, the same by nature but that birth and fortune has made a distinction!!

Shock and horror at the terrible scenes the priests were witnessing, combined with a feeling of frustration at their own helplessness. This was followed by frantic appeals, in the hope that if the sufferings of the people were known, relief would come. The contrast with better times struck many of them especially at the approach of Christmas. The multitude, Fr Patrick Byrne from Gort recorded, were 'dying a slow but *dire death*'. 'How I wish the real sufferings of the people could reach the ears of the rich of this life', wrote Flannelly from Clifden. 'Ballintubber is *gone*, alas!,' lamented its parish priest, James Browne. 'My fine virtuous, holy people have been starved to death. The landlords of all sects and creed have conspired for their destruction – the Catholic Landlords the most cruelly disposed. *We* are *ourselves* nearly reduced to the level of our people.'

The landlords, however, were in difficulties. They were no longer able to collect rents, but were still obliged by law to

support an increasing number of destitute in their Poor Law
Union. Russell and much of British public opinion tended to
scapegoat them and the clamour increased in the latter years
of the famine to make 'Irish property' (the landlords) support
'Irish poverty'. The aim of the Poor Law Extension Act of
1847 was to shift more of the burden of supporting the poor
from the general exchequer to the local landlords. Many
landlords – like Lord Kingston, Viscount Gort, Lord Dufferin,
the Duke of Devonshire, Lord Cloncurry, Richard Devereux
of Wexford, Lord Lurgan, the Erringtons of Kingston, Sir
Arthur Brooke, the Adairs in Antrim and others – were very
generous to their tenants. In Cavan, Lord Farnham worked
together with Bishop Browne in organising relief and in
Donegal, the united efforts of landlords and clergy (Anglican,
Catholic and Presbyterian) lessened the suffering consider-
ably. Many landlords, however, evicted unrelentingly. The
clergy, eyewitnesses of heart-rending scenes, no longer minc-
ing their language, called them 'exterminators' of the people.
Archbishop Slattery of Cashel complained of an 'extermination going on under the protection of the law'. Bishop French
of Kilmacduagh denounced 'the Extermination' and Bishop
Keating of Kildare and Leighlin, forced by government pressure to censure a priest of his diocese for speaking out, admitted
that all the priest was doing was protesting against 'the
Extermination'. The word was to take on a greater significance when, at the Synod of Thurles in 1850, the assembled
bishops used it to describe the evictions.

'Rotting in Heaps on the Shores of the Stranger'

One of the results of evictions and hunger was an enormous
increase in emigration, sometimes voluntary, sometimes organised and assisted by the landlords to clear their land.
Many emigrants survived and prospered, but many never
reached the land of their hopes. Many died at Liverpool, one
of the main ports for those going to stay in Britain or on their
way to America, and of the priests ministering to them, some

ten succumbed to the deadly fever. More haunting still were the scenes at Grosse Île, a place and a name forever linked with the Irish Famine. Grosse Île, an island in the middle of the great Saint Laurence river and some thirty miles from Quebec, had been set aside by the Canadian government as the quarantine island for immigrants and, since the fare to Canada was lower than the fare to New York and the regulations governing the transport of passengers less strict, most of the Irish who emigrated during the Famine disembarked there. Some did not make it to the island; many perished at sea: of the 476 passengers from Major Mahon's estate in County Roscommon, who embarked on the *Virginius* at Liverpool, 158 died at sea and those who survived the voyage of death, were, in the words of Dr George Douglas, the Canadian medical officer at Grosse Île, no more than 'ghastly yellow looking spectres' and 'not more than six or eight really healthy or able to exert themselves'.

Because of the ice, the Saint Laurence river was navigable only from May to the beginning of November. In 1847 the first ship with Irish emigrants arrived on 14 May. The Catholic and Anglican clergy were quick to come to their aid and both handed over their churches to serve as extra hospitals. The Celtic Cross on the island records the names of forty-four priests who ministered to the Famine victims. Surprisingly, many of the priests had Irish names – James Nelligan, James McDevitt, Hugh McGurk, James McDonnell, Michael O'Reilly, Michael Kerrigan, John Caulfield O'Grady, Edward Horan, William Dunne, and Michael Power – and a number of them were born in Ireland. Twenty priests caught the Famine fever and six died; seven Anglican clergymen caught the fever and two died, as well as four doctors and other helpers. To diminish the risk of mortality among his priests working in Grosse Île, Archbishop Signay wisely decided to rotate his priests, asking them to stay only a week at a time on the island. Many volunteered to stay much longer or returned a second or third time. Fr Bernard McGauran of Notre Dame de Québec, was the first priest to go there, at the head of a group of seminary professors from the Séminaire de Québec. McGauran, a young man of 25, recently ordained, was from Ballisodare in County Sligo. He caught the fever but recovered and returned again to spend in all eighty days on the island.

The archbishop, deeply concerned about the emigrants' plight, brought priests from all over his diocese and soon seven were serving at the same time on the island. When, in July 1847, the parish of Rimouski petitioned that their curate, Fr Antoine Lebel, not be sent to Grosse Île, the archbishop made a considered reply through his secretary and chancellor, Fr Charles-Félix Cazeau: 'He (Archbishop Signay) greatly regrets that he finds himself in a position where he must expose his priests to death in sending them to the sick detained at the quarantine station; but he regrets even more letting a large number of people die without spiritual recourse – people who have become part of his diocesan flock and, thrust into an abyss of affliction, are in such dire need of the immortal consolation that religion can bring. You will therefore not find it a bad thing that Mr Lebel ... share in the merit of a good number of his colleagues who hastened to respond to the invitation that they were given to go, at the peril of their lives, to prepare the last moments of the dying ... This man (Fr Lebel) would be embarrassed should the attachment that his Rimouski parishioners have for him, deprive him of the honour of devoting his turn to a ministry that calls for a true minister of Jesus Christ.'

The pastoral priority of the archbishop in this and similar letters is striking. The sick and dying Irish were 'people who have become part of his diocesan flock' and, since they were in greater need, he was resolved to call to their assistance, priests from all over his vast diocese even if it meant taking them away from other important work, or incurring local displeasure. The Anglican Bishop of Montreal, George Jehoshaphat Mountain, was equally solicitous for the emigrants and paid two visits to the island, officiating at twenty-two burials.

The distress of the emigrants was awful. Fr McGauran in his first letter to the archbishop, on 24 May 1847, recounted his experience:

> Today I spent five hours in the hold of one of these (ships) where I administered the sacraments to a hundred people, while my very welcome colleague was on board another … While we are on the ships, there are people dying in the hospital without the sacraments. I have not taken off my surplice today: we meet people everywhere in need of the sacraments; they are dying on the rocks, and on the beach where they have been cast by the sailors who simply could not carry them to the hospitals. We buried twenty-eight yesterday, twenty-eight today, and now (two hours past midnight), there are thirty dead whom we will bury tomorrow. I have not gone to bed for five nights. The spectacle, My Lord, is heart-rending. Once these hapless people are struck down by this strange malady, they lose all mental and physical powers and die in the most acute agony! We hardly give anyone Holy Communion, because we do not have the time … I am not at all afraid of the fever, I have never felt happier than in my actual state. The Master Whom I serve holds me in His all powerful Hand … We can hardly stop to take a rest, but someone comes in haste to summon us. There are already a great number of orphans, whom I recommend to your Grace … My Lord, it is impossible that two priests will do, my legs are beginning to bother me, because I am always on my feet.

McGauran made one major observation which, if it had been acted on early in the season, would have reduced the number of deaths. While admitting that the hospitals on the island filled up quickly, he complained that Dr Douglas, the medical officer in charge 'forces the captains to keep them on board, and we have at present thirty-two of these vessels which are like floating hospitals, where death makes frightful inroads, and the sick are crowded in among the more healthy, with the result that all are victims to this terrible sickness.' His complaint was justified. Ship captains told Father Elzéar-Alexandre Taschereau, later Archbishop of Quebec, 'that they have had three and ten times more deaths here at the anchorage in their vessels than during all the voyage'. In this letter of 3 June to Archbishop Signay, Taschereau went on to make the chilling comment: 'it is a very painful thing to say and even more difficult to believe, but it is, in my opinion, the expression of the truth, spoken by a captain whom I met today: "It would be better just to send a battery of artillery from Quebec, to sink these ships to the bottom rather than let all these poor people die in such an agonising manner: if things don't change, they will all die"'. At the official inquiry into the management of Grosse Île held later in the year, it was admitted that far more died on the ships than on the shore; many who were healthy when they reached port caught disease from being cooped up with the dying and the dead. Fr William Wallace, later rector of Fordham University, told the inquiry: 'I ... observed to Orderly Smith, that there was a corpse in the same bed with a patient, and his reply was that in those cases they were left until the following morning.' At one stage there was a two-mile long queue of forty ships awaiting permission to discharge their passengers.

Even getting to visit the emigrants was a problem. Pleading for the use of a row-boat, the Galway-born priest, Bernard O'Reilly, recounted: 'Vessels came daily crowded with sick, and unless some person, through kindness, bring us on board, the wretched Emigrants are allowed to die in the sight of their Clergy, without the supreme consolation of an Irish Catholic, the last rites of his church.' The conditions on the ships were appalling. 'How can we wish them health,' wrote an appalled Father Taschereau, 'when all breathe the foul air of the between-decks, walk on flooring covered with muck; consider the unwholesome food and dirty water they take for their meals! Most of them have for a bed the boards or a few filthy wisps of straw that do more harm than good ... how many more after a month and a half of the crossing, are wearing the same clothes and the same shoes they had when they had come on board ..., and which they have not taken off day or night? I have seen people whose feet were so stuck to their socks that I could not anoint them!' The sailors sometimes refused to go down into the fever-ridden holds and some brave captains had to carry the sick and dead out themselves. The dead were often lifted off the ships with grappling hooks. Father Hubert Robson, who is reputed to have said, 'I will give my life if I must for those unfortunates', also went down into the filthy holds where, walking ankle-deep in slime and filth, he loaded the sick on his shoulders and carried them to the hospital. He died of the fever on 1 July.

On shore, the sick were lodged in tents, sheds and in the Catholic and Protestant Chapels. In some sheds the beds were placed one tier above the other. Father O'Reilly appealed to the Special Committee to remove the upper tier since the sick person found it almost impossible to clamber down and once down found it still more difficult to climb back. His description was horrifying: 'I saw an unfortunate invalid, who, after having thus descended from a bed about five foot ... above the ground, lay extended at full length, and imploringly appealed to the pity of the others to lift and place him again in his bed; besides, the excrements arising from the dysentery of the sick frequently descend from the upper tier on the unfortunates in the lower tier.'

Appalled at the misery and suffering, Archbishop Signay wrote to warn the Irish Bishops that 'the scenes of horror and desolation of which the chaplains are daily and ocular witnesses, almost stagger belief and baffle description.' On the other side of the Atlantic, Bishop Maginn of Derry, angrily complained that 'the bravest of our country (are) rotting in heaps on the shores of the stranger' and laid the blame on government indifference.

The official number of emigrants buried at Grosse Île in 1847 alone is 5,424 and throughout Canada, it is estimated that 12,000 Irish died. In Montreal, seventeen Sisters of Charity, or 'Grey Nuns', seven priests and the Mayor of the city, John Mills; in Toronto, Bishop Michael Power, and Fr McInerney, the parish priest of Lachine. Catholic and Anglican clergy remarked on how grateful the dying were to receive their attention. The French-Canadian Fr Tascherau wrote: 'they welcome us with open arms everywhere. The blessings they give us and their marks of affection are so lively and so cordial that they fill us with courage and consolation.' In Ireland Bishop French had similar experiences of the simple gratitude of the sick and dying.

Some thousands of children lost both mother and father. 'The number of orphans is very great,' wrote Fr Tascherau, 'and sadly enough we could not do anything more for them than to entrust them to a few mothers of families and give them some money ... Most will die ... happy not to have known their misfortune here ... I saw a child playing with the hand of his mother who had just died.' Before long, Fr Cazeau, diocesan chancellor and, from 1850, vicar-general, took charge of the orphans. They were brought to Quebec, where many of them were looked after by the Societé Charitable des Dames de Québec, and later by the Grey Nuns. Many priests, hearing of the tragic state of the children, travelled the long distances from towns like Rimouski, in Gaspésie, to bring them to their parishes where they were adopted by French-Canadian families.

The part played by the church, from Italy to Belgium in the old world, and from Canada to Australia in the new, showed it at its best in its use of its world-wide organisation. No previous relief activity for disaster or famine had attracted such widespread, almost universal, reaction. In the United Kingdom and the United States, the Quakers' organisation played an important part. In Europe, the interest that Daniel

O'Connell's career had aroused over the previous decades was also important. For the whole Catholic world, Pius IX's Encyclical, *Praedecessores Nostros*, was of the greatest significance, for, it galvanised bishops all over the world to send aid and, as letters to Murray forwarding relief-monies recounted, its publication aroused great and active sympathy for Ireland. Of major importance, too, and of significance for the future, were the Irish abroad who, mainly through their clergy, mobilised relief. Important though this was in Europe, it was far more important in the new countries – the British Empire, the United States, South America – where a network of Irish clergy had grown up to cater for the Irish abroad. It is also a first indication of the growing influence of the Irish church throughout the British Empire and in the United States. In Canada, it was not merely a question of raising funds but of coping with a mass of refugees. The churches, for their part, rose to the challenge.

CHAPTER 3

1847-8 Assassinations and Rebellion

The Silence of the Church?

Despite their work in ministering to the Famine-stricken, the clergy came in for criticism. Sometimes their parishioners blamed them for failing to obtain aid. A Mayo priest, Francis Keogh, complaining that 'I have nothing for my poor people' who were angry at his failure to obtain relief, fled from his parish and took refuge with another priest. It was only when he received relief funds that he was able to return. Allegations that Laurence O'Sullivan, parish priest of Goleen, County Cork, abandoned his parish, are discounted in recent research, but Richard Webb, a Quaker, reported that Tom Welsh, a priest in Erris, County Mayo, was selfish and dishonest and abhorred by his people. After 1848, his name is no longer found in the *Catholic Directory*. At the beginning of 1847, Elizabeth Smith of Baltiboys, County Wicklow, complained that the parish priest refused to supervise the store at Blackditches, although since she was engaged in a long-running feud with him on schooling, her complaint may not be objective. Louisa Moore of Moore Hall, who wanted women to be on the relief committees, believed that some parish priests in good parishes did not contribute enough to the relief work.

More challenging was the criticism made by *The Nation*, the organ of Young Ireland, in July 1847:

> Independent of their local duties, which they have discharged with a devotion unsurpassed in the annals of martyrdom, have they in their political capacity, as ... citizens, raised their voices against the murder of their people ... ? Or

have they ... backed the abettors of that infamous policy
which gave to the butcher two million of their flock? Have
they whispered when they should have denounced, or
been silent when they should have thundered?

This was a serious charge. Since many attributed the massive
mortality to the non-interventionist policy of the government, the inference was that the church, through its silence,
allowed it to happen. The allegation evoked angry refuta-
tions. James Fitzpatrick, parish priest of Castletownroche,
County Cork, wrote:

> Did this gentleman ever read any of the thousand letters
> of the Catholic priesthood, complaining of the murder of
> their parishioners by starvation? ... The Catholic clergy
> took every opportunity, publicly and privately, of de-
> nouncing the criminal policy of the Whigs, whereby mil-
> lions starved to death. What more could we do? And after
> this we are accused of being abettors of murder, and to
> have stimulated to crime.

This no-win situation in which the clergy found itself also an-
gered the fiery Fr James Maher, of Killeshan: 'How could they
save the Hecatomb sacrificed at Bantry?' he asked. 'If they
raise their voice against oppression they run the risk of being
accused of exciting to murder.' Many bishops, although further removed from the people than their priests, had spoken
up. Archbishop MacHale, shocked by Russell's announce-
ment in August 1846 of a switch to a policy of non-intervent-
ion, immediately warned the Prime Minister that 'You might
as well at once issue an edict of general starvation ... ' After
the calamity of Black '47, MacHale, grimly recalling Russell's
promises at the outset of the Famine, wrote, with biting sar-
casm: 'How ungrateful of the Catholics of Ireland not to pour
forth canticles of gratitude to the ministers who promised
that none of them should perish and then suffered 2 million
to starve.' Archbishop Slattery came out publicly in June
1848: 'The distress was such that I could not resist the imposition

of my voice on behalf of the Poor of Christ.' Bishop Ryan of Limerick denounced the higher classes for being 'cold and callous to the voice of humanity ... untouched by the cries of famine and pestilence, the wailings of hunger, the lamentations of women and children'. The Irish-born Bishop of New York, John Hughes, in a remarkable lecture delivered in New York on 20 March 1847, analysed and rejected the prevailing system of political economy whose high priest he saw as Lord John Russell. Government intervention, he argued, was crucial. Since there was, he believed, no general scarcity of food in Ireland, the rights of life were dearer and higher than the rights of property. For Hughes, 'political economy' was the murderer of the Famine-stricken and he castigated Russell for his alleged statement 'that nothing prevented him from employing government vessels to carry bread to a starving people, except his unwillingness to disturb the current of trade'.

The Bishops and Collective Action

These powerful comments were made by individuals; a collective criticism did not come until the autumn of 1847. Apart from the dilemma highlighted by Fitzpatrick and Maher, it was understandable that in the first year of the Liberal government whose return to power O'Connell had welcomed, the clergy had every reason to believe that Russell, the champion of justice to Ireland, would prove, in Murray's words, another 'Joseph'. At first, too, each bishop experienced the disaster as it occurred in his own diocese, and did not think of the Famine in national terms and they, no more than the government, could not have anticipated a disaster on the scale of Black '47. Furthermore, the Catholic Church, although the church of 80 per cent of the people, existed in the context of a Protestant state, which still regarded it with suspicion. This made older bishops, in particular, circumspect in voicing criticism.

A committee of Meath priests wrote to the hierarchy in 1848,

suggesting another reason why the bishops were slow in taking collective action. It was a courageous and critical letter.
After praising the work for the Famine-stricken of 'each of
your lordships in his own diocese', the committee felt 'co-
erced to give expression to the opinion of the clergy and laity,
that had your lordships, with irresistible unanimity ... taken
that position between the starving people and their rulers,
the poor would not have been neglected as they were'. It
went on to make a challenging comment: 'If this omission
were owing ... to the want of unanimity on other subjects
among your lordships, which has of late years become so
painfully public, this committee indulges the fond hope that
the distressing want of union, for the sake of the poor ... shall
cease for ever.' The Meath priests had identified a problem,
which was, at least, a contributory factor to the dilemma; the
bishops were more divided than they had been for decades.
Recent governments had offered Catholics concessions especially on education, both primary and university, partly as a
genuine reform, partly with a view to wean Catholics away
from O'Connell's movement for Repeal of the Union.
Important though these concessions were, they were also,
from a Catholic and nationalist viewpoint, flawed and so,
while some bishops, like Murray of Dublin, trusted the government, the majority, led by MacHale of Tuam and Slattery of
Cashel, remained suspicious of its intentions. The disagree-
ments between them became sharp and public and had
sowed distrust. As the Meath committee suspected, this hin-
dered united action. The bishops' disunity surfaced even on
the question of relief monies from the pope and foreign
Catholic bishops, which Murray and William Crolly,
Archbishop of Armagh, wanted to hand into the Relief
Committee in Dublin. Murray explained his reasons to
Cullen, rector of the Irish College in Rome:

> Many people thought that, if it had been distributed
> through the Central General Committee, it would have
> been more creditable to Rome, as having less of an exclusive

appearance, and more of the spirit of the Good Samaritan; whereas Protestants were subscribing immense sums to be applied principally, indeed almost entirely, for the relief of Catholics.

Slattery and MacHale, however, insisted that the monies be sent to the archbishops, who would then distribute them directly to the other bishops, a view Cullen supported. Murray was forced to accept it. Although Murray's view shows a greater sensitivity towards the Protestant churches, it was understandable, too, that the Archbishops of Tuam and Cashel, were unwilling that monies expressly donated for the Catholic poor should be handed over to a mixed committee. Protestant Evangelicals had stepped up their missions to convert Famine-stricken Catholics and religious tensions were rising. Furthermore, the bishops believed they could distribute the money quicker and better than any committee in faraway Dublin. Already, however, before the Meath priests had appealed to them, the hierarchy had taken concerted action.

'Rights of Property versus Rights of Life'

In the autumn of 1847, shocked by the distress, the bishops determined on concerted action. Their annual meeting was not due until November, but believing the situation too grave to wait until then, they met in Dublin on 18 October and drew up the strongest memorial they had ever presented to government, sharply criticising its policies and raising issues which they never before dared to broach.

The bishops complained that the government's relief measures were wholly inadequate. The workhouses were overcrowded and fever-ridden, and the grim choice facing the people was of starving if they did not enter them and dying of disease if they did. Turning to the cause of the Famine, the bishops rejected out of hand the view, widely held in England, that it was the 'innate indolence' of the Irish people. The real causes, they insisted, were 'unjust penal enactments

... which ... deprived the ... bulk of the people of the rights to property thus debarring them from the enjoyment of its fruits ... If the labourer is worthy of his hire', they declared, 'an axiom of natural as well as of revealed religion ... it would be a violation of those sacred maxims to appropriate the entire crop of the husbandman without compensation for the seed or the labour.' In Ireland, however, they pointed out, laws 'sanctioning such unnatural injustice ... not only exist but are extensively enforced with reckless and unrelenting vigour.' While carefully affirming the rights of property, the bishops insisted that there existed a prior and more fundamental right:

> The sacred and indefeasible rights of life are forgotten amidst the incessant reclamations of the subordinate rights of property ... Hallowed as are the rights of property those of life are still more sacred, and rank as such in every well regulated scale (of values) that adjusts the relative possessions of man; and if this scale had not been frequently reversed we should not have so often witnessed in those heart-rending scenes of the eviction of the tenantry, the oppressions that are done under the sun, the tears of the innocent having no comforter, and unable to resist violence, being destitute of help from any.

This refusal to blame the Famine on the laziness of the peasants and the insistence on the primacy of the right to life over the 'subordinate' rights of property, amounted to a vigorous defence of the poor. The bishops' memorial achieved nothing. The viceroy made a polite reply, promising that the government would act to protect life while at the same time he wrote to Russell denouncing the violent nature of the memorial. This he attributed to Archbishop MacHale and, anxious to win him over, he opened a correspondence with him. MacHale replied in very moderate tones explaining how difficult it was for the clergy to maintain calm when the people were starving before their eyes. Impressed by MacHale's conciliatory tone, Clarendon reported delightedly to Russell that if he could help MacHale feed his people in Connacht, he would win over the fiery archbishop. Within a few weeks, however, a major row had erupted between the clergy and the authorities and the promising correspondence between viceroy and archbishop went no further.

Accomplices of Assassins?

On Tuesday, 2 November 1847, Major Denis Mahon was shot dead on his way home to Strokestown House. Mahon, a handsome young cavalry officer of the 9th Lancers, had inherited the badly-managed Hartland estate in County Roscommon and proposed to buy out the tenants, offering them a passage to Canada. Only a minority accepted and, as the rest would 'neither pay nor go', he evicted over 3,000 of them including, it was alleged, 84 widows. His murder, one of a half-dozen murders or attempted murders of landlords or their agents during the autumn of 1847, alarmed the landed gentry. In the House of Lords, Lord Farnham of Farnham in Cavan, alleged that the parish priest of Strokestown, Michael McDermott, had declared at the Sunday Mass previous to the murder that 'Major Mahon is worse than Cromwell and yet he lives'. Farnham's remarks caused a sensation, his words were taken as proof and parliament and the press resounded with fierce denunciations of the priests as abettors of assassination. For Lord Clarendon, the new viceroy, an alarmist who had shut himself up in the viceregal lodge, these murders were proof that 'servile war (that is, a revolt of the slaves) against all landlords and English rule' was about to break out. He redoubled his frantic calls for a special powers act. Russell, the prime minister, for whom the landlords were the villains, and their evictions of the tenants 'lynch law', replied sharply that:

> It is quite true that landlords in England would not like to be shot like hares and partridges. But neither does any landlord in England turn out fifty persons at once, and

burn their houses over their heads, giving them no provision for the future. The murders are atrocious, so are the ejectments.

British public opinion, however, accepted Farnham's allegation. Fr McDermott indignantly denied the charges, and assured the public 'by the most solemn asseverations a clergyman can utter, that ... Major Mahon was never denounced, nor even his name mentioned from any Chapel altar ... on any Sunday before his death'. *The Times* of London denounced McDermott's denial as an evasion of the truth for if he did not do it on Sunday, he could have done it on Monday, which was a holy day. It rejected his challenge for legal process alleging that 'his congregation (was) prepared to perjure themselves in platoons to save their spiritual instructor from the gallows'. A further embitterment came when Lord Shrewsbury, a leading English Catholic peer, accepted, without further proof, the allegations of connivance at assassination and duplicity levelled against McDermott. Responsibility for the Famine deaths, which MacHale and other clerics blamed on the government, Shrewsbury attributed to the 'unerring, though inscrutable designs of God'. The Irish were to blame, too, he said, 'for God's visitation was grievously aggravated by their ingratitude', because 'every ... expression of gratitude has been withheld both from the government and the people of England'. The assassinations were 'part of one great conspiracy against property'. Lord Palmerston, the foreign secretary, declared that the best way to put a stop to assassinations of landlords was to hang the local priest, an opinion which others voiced too. He instructed Lord Minto, the British minister on a special mission in Italy, to tell Pius IX that 'Major Mahon who was shot the other day was denounced by his priest at the altar the Sunday before ... That denunciation ... made all the people in the neighbourhood think the deed a holy one.'

Was the charge genuine? Priests sometimes abused their

power and intimidated or bullied their parishioners. Some priests did make denunciations from the altar, a very serious abuse which bishops through synodal legislation and other means were attempting to stamp out. Yet no grounds existed for the claim made by Palmerston and others that Mac-Dermott's guilt was well established. A score of respectable parishioners solemnly swore that he had never denounced Mahon. Alarmed at the accusations, McDermott's bishop, George Browne of Elphin, went to Strokestown to investigate. 'The result of my inquiries,' he affirmed, 'has been that he had not on Sunday, Monday, ferial or holy day, not at any time nor in any place directly nor indirectly denounced Major Mahon.'

Privately, too, Clarendon told his friend Reeve of *The Times*: 'I have in vain tried by every means in my power to get such (evidence of MacDermott's involvement) and Ross Mahon, the Major's cousin and agent who has been doing the same at the place, admitted that the reports were so various and conflicting that he himself had no notion of what McD(ermott) actually did.' The undersecretary to the government, Thomas Redington, who as a Catholic and a Connacht landlord would have access to information, also failed to find evidence against the priest. When the murder trial took place in July 1848, it transpired that the murder had been planned before the Sunday when McDermott was supposed to have denounced Mahon from the pulpit. Two men were executed and others transported, but McDermott's name did not figure at the trial.

What is certain is that, after Mahon's arrival from England, he and the priest had disagreed sharply at the September meeting of the Strokestown Relief Committee. Mahon's account of the dispute was that he had questioned the eligibility of some persons for relief and that McDermott angrily accused Mahon of tyrannising over him, alleging that 'I had spent my winter in London to amuse myself and had left my people to starve in the streets and die'. Mahon was clear about the issue involved: it was 'that whatever I did with regard to my property, I conceived, rested with myself, and that I would not allow him or any man to interfere with me in that respect ...' McDermott gave his explanation of why Mahon was shot: 'The sole ... cause' was 'the infamous and inhuman cruelties which were wantonly and unnecessarily exercised against a tenantry, whose feelings were already wound up to woeful and vengeful exasperation by the loss of their exiled relatives, as well as by hunger and pestilence'. The 'loss of their exiled relatives' is a reference to a rumour that the ship carrying the evicted had foundered. This rumour was false, but the ship, the *Virginius*, was one of the worst of the 'coffin ships'. The contrast in outlook between landlord and priest, which comes through so sharply in those statements – one with its determination to protect his lawful property rights, the other raging at 'infamous cruelty' and people starving on the streets – constitutes a thought-provoking commentary on the conflicting attitudes that influenced reactions to the great calamity of the Famine!

British public opinion as expressed particularly in *The Times*, *Punch*, and Parliament, kept up a fierce denunciation of the priests as instigators of murder. It provoked a sharp counter-reaction. Priests engaged in relief work, in visiting the dying and, especially, exhorting the people to resignation and calm, were appalled at what they saw as slander. From Cavan, Philip Foy, curate at Shercock, complained that 'in this diocese (Kilmore), on the express order of our venerated prelate, every clergyman reprobated those scandalous secret societies of Ribbonmen and Molly Maguires simultaneously last October in every chapel before the slanders were even thought of.' He added bitterly, however, that it was 'hard to teach patience to a man who sees his father and mother or wife and children driven from the houses of their ancestors, to the bogs and ditches, to starvation and death.' Fr Maher of Killeshan, denouncing the sixteen ounces of food doled out to the poor in Carlow Poorhouse, savagely commented on an article in the London *Times*:

> *The Times* ... describes the priest as 'sending his thug upon a sacred mission, blessing his weapon and absolving him beforehand of the seeming crime'. Introduce the workhouse dietary of Carlow into England, and will *The Times* tell us how many murders, without sacerdotal prompting, it would produce in a season? ... Talk indeed of a conspiracy against life! Here (in the workhouse) we have it ...

Palmerston's Roman diplomacy, however, achieved some success. On 3 January 1848, at the Pope's request, Cardinal Fransoni, the secretary of the Congregation of Propaganda, sent a reproachful letter to the Irish archbishops, referring to rumours in the press that the clergy approved of murders and demanding a full account. The reaction this evoked made Palmerston's victory a pyrrhic one, for it set the nationalists, priests and laity, wild with anger. Remonstrances poured in and protest meetings were held. If Propaganda wanted full information, more than one bishop was prepared to provide it. Bishop Maginn of Derry, in a letter that has some of the resonance of modern-day Liberation Theology, appealed to Archbishop Crolly, the Catholic primate, to defend the clergy to the pope:

> No clergyman has transgressed the bounds of Christian duty, which makes it incumbent on every follower of the Redeemer to stand by the oppressed against their oppressors – for the poor and the needy against those that strip them. An ardent love of country for which our great pope himself is so distinguished could not be reputed an inordinate zeal for *factious* pursuits. A desire to promote by *peaceful* and *constitutional* means, the amelioration of our *unhappy country* made by *misrule* the most wretched on *earth*, could not be considered a 'political pursuit' – nor could in fine the praiseworthy efforts of our clergy to check the proselytiser ... nor their earnest efforts ... to bring public

opinion to bear on the ruthless extermination of their helpless starving hearers, through any malversion, be deemed criminal in them.

Maginn and his clergy, who also went out of their way to praise good landlords in their diocese of Derry, resolved to keep a register in each parish of the acts of cruelty of landlords! Other bishops also wrote, and Paul Cullen, rector of the Irish College, who was highly regarded in Rome and understood Roman ways better than most, conducted an energetic supporting action. The elderly Bishop of Kilmacduagh and Kilfenora, Edmund French, took up his pen to defend his priests, recounting to Cullen the appalling situation:

> the yellings of the poor, on the roads, in the streets of our towns, at all our houses …, the heart-rending scenes in the houses of the poor, lying sick of fever, starvation, of inanition and want, are the daily prospects of our clergy … In one parish alone there were twenty-one deaths of heads of families in four days … they all died with the utmost resignation to the Will of God, blessing the priest for a very small temporary help. These are the constant scenes constantly witnessed by our clergy in the south and west of Ireland! and alas if we dare describe these afflictions of our people and our own agonies at their heartrending sufferings, we are stamped by our enemies of this English press and the leading Members of Parliament as surplissed (sic) ruffians and instigators of the murder of the landed gentry and the exterminators of the people! 'O, how false are these accusations,' French exclaimed, 'as God knows and only knows'. French, who was timid and scrupulous, avoided the political arena and the moving account he gave is all the more credible.

Fiercer far was a thirty-one page letter that Archbishop Slattery wrote to Rome. He summed up the situation thus:

> The Catholic clergy being the only persons to stand for-

ward against the oppression of the people, the landlords availed themselves of the national bigotry of England to raise the cry of murder against them, to turn away public attention from the numberless murders caused by themselves. Hence the calumnies sanctioned by the government to forward their own purposes of blackening us in the eyes of Europe and even of Rome, thereby to destroy the liberty of our church.

Slattery insisted that the clergy, on the one hand, were the only support the people had, and, on the other, the preservers of peace in the country. English clergy, principally Bishop Briggs of the northern district, and the Rosminian, Fr Pagani, felt just as indignant at the denunciation of the Irish clergy. Suspecting a government plot to discredit and dominate the church, they supported the Irish bishops fully in their protests and Briggs went so far as to draw up the draft of a strong protest which he sent to the Irish bishops for submission to Rome. Finally, on 27 March 1848, in a joint protest, seventeen of the twenty-seven Irish bishops replied to Pius IX's request for information on Palmerston's charge of incitation to assassination. Their letter was extraordinarily bitter. The accusers of the clergy, they said, were 'modern pharisees', 'a true brood of vipers, with the venom of asps', who whispered calumnies against priests and bishops. Then, interpreting the attacks on the clergy and the attempt to impose the Queen's Colleges, as part of a government plot to control the church, they sent two of their number to Rome to counteract it. Rome, under such pressure, hastened to write to the indignant bishops reassuring them of its complete confidence.

1848 – The Year of Revolutions!

The furore about assassinations revealed how deep-rooted the distrust between the governing class in England and Irish Catholics had become. It sheds light, too, on the attitude of some Irish clergy when, in that extraordinary year of 1848, revolutions broke out all over Europe. In February, a revolution in France toppled King Louis-Philippe, and it was followed by revolutions in Italy, Germany, Austria, Hungary and elsewhere. The revolutionaries were well-disposed to religion and many clergy sided with the revolution; in France, Bishop Parisis declared that henceforth Christianity would claim for its own those sublime words – Liberty, Equality, Fraternity; in Milan, Cardinal Archbishop Romilli took his place at the barricades; in Rome, the patriotic Pius IX's cry, 'God bless Italy', appeared to Italians to be a blessing on those seeking to unite Italy which meant expelling the Austrians.

Before long many Irish priests began to take a similar stand. In Limerick, on 3 April, Rev Dr Michael O'Brien promised that the priests would 'brave any danger to wrest their (their countrymen's) souls and bodies from the debasement, destitution, and destruction of foreign rule.' The following day in Waterford, Father Nicholas Coughlan declared that the social contract between people and government was broken:

> England's treatment of us for the past two years would abundantly prove that there is *practically* no government in this kingdom, and, therefore, in conscience, no allegiance is further due ... (I)n allegiance there is a contract, and ... should either party fail to supply the due conditions, then it falls to the ground ... it is pretty clear that *one* of the contracting parties was found wanting. The unworthy death of some 800,000 honest men attest it ... And, as to this heavy scourge coming from holy Providence, I believe none of it; I rather believe it comes *from beyond the (Irish) channel* ...

Other priests also insisted that the existing social contract had been broken. A Limerick priest declared that it was 'far better to die as men died in Berlin, Vienna, and Paris than that another million should die the death of Skibbereen'. Fr Owen O'Sullivan, the parish priest of Killorglin, took a far stronger view. At a Repeal meeting in Killarney attended by seven priests, he was reported as declaring:

Louis-Philippe was a bad man and therefore a determined people armed and hurled him from the pinnacle of greatness. But, bad though he was, no man in France died of famine. Was that the case under the 'base, bloody, and brutal Whigs'? Seek the answer from the millions of our poor countrymen who are rotting in their graves because of the misrule of England ...

If their constitutional appeal (were) treated with ridicule, he said, he for one ... was prepared to take his stand with the people.

More succinctly another priest cried: 'Up with the barricades and invoke the God of battles', while Fr John Kenyon advised: 'Make your peace with God and arm quietly'!

Bishop Maginn denounced the government as solely concerned with the maintenance of law and order and indifferent to the ruin and death of the people:

our merchants bankrupt, our farmers ... beggars, the bravest of our country rotting in heaps on the shores of the stranger and the remainder ... gaunt spectres flitting over ... the loveliest land on earth ... at every elbow a spy or informer ... tens of thousands of military or police ingloriously watching the convulsions and writhings of the starving victims of misrule, lest, in their agony, the slightest symptom of disaffection should pass unnoticed or unpunished ... Sooner than allow the misery of my people to continue, like the Archbishop of Milan, I would rather grasp the cross and the green flag of Ireland and rescue my country, or perish with its people.

Most bishops, however, led by Murray of Dublin, tried, and with success, to keep their priests from involvement in rebellion and Murray went so far as to issue a statement to the press appealing to the people to have no part in it. Recalling his own fearful experiences of 1798, (when only by climbing out the back window of the church did he escape from the Orange yeomanry who had brought a cannon up to the door of the chapel in Arklow), he asked 'Can anyone be surprised that a thrill of horror should rush through my soul at the thought of the recurrence of such a calamity? May God in his mercy avert it.'

The turning-point, however, came when a further more radical revolution broke out in Paris and Archbishop Affre was shot at the barricades in June 1848. Catholics in France and elsewhere turned against the Revolution and the Irish clergy, influenced by a press which the viceroy manipulated successfully, abandoned any revolutionary ideas they had. When the Young Ireland rebellion broke out in July, they advised against what was a hopeless struggle. For this they were criticised by Young Irelanders, including the leader, Smith O'Brien, who said that the people 'preferred to die of starvation ... rather than to fight for their lives and liberties' and implied that the bishops were in great part responsible. Yet, apart from the question of the moral justification of rebelling, the pathetic, ill-prepared nature of the 'rebellion' gave good reason to the clergy for persuading the totally unequipped and half-starved peasants to go home. Fr Philip Fitzgerald, who, at Ballingarry where the only action took place, rode up to Smith O'Brien to persuade him to abandon the attack on the police, later explained his reasons:

> that there should be carnage at all was much to be lamented, but that it should be ... especially on the side of a poor and oppressed population, with whom all my sympathies were enlisted, and with whom I in every way identified, was an idea from which I recoiled instinctively.

Renehan, president of Maynooth College, told Bishop Kennedy of Killaloe that the Young Irelanders were the 'seducers of the people to the gallows or a bloody grave'. Later nationalists felt the priests had saved the people from a slaughter as great as that of 1798.

For the priests there was an important aftermath to the rebellion. The government, believing that people had lost faith in their clergy for flinching from a rebellion which they had appeared to encourage, and knowing the poverty-stricken state to which the Famine had reduced many of them, seized this moment to offer the clergy a state salary. In the past, nationalists, both priests and people, rejected such offers, fearing them as attempts to divide the clergy from the people. Poorly-circumstanced as the priests now were, would they maintain the same opposition? Some, particularly the bishops, opposed it. Archbishop Murray and Archdeacon O'Sullivan made a reasoned case for accepting it, remarking that it was all very well for the bishops to refuse payment, but the poor curates were starving. In the privacy of his diary O'Sullivan added: 'The bishops lose no opportunity in recording their determination of resisting it, but this is because they have not the trouble of wringing it out of the miserable creatures from whom we are obliged to extract it.' 'The poor people,' he noted, 'certainly are willing to contribute to our support as far as their means will allow them.' O'Sullivan's concern was that the people were poorly instructed and the reason for that was the shortage of priests and the reason for the shortage of priests was the lack of money to support them. 'The number of priests to attend to them (the people) is too small ... with a population of over 10,000 and an area of near 60,000 statute acres, how could myself and my curates come at all the calls, and attend to the instruction of the people?'

At their meeting in November 1848, the bishops took a unanimous decision. Underlining their solidarity with their people, they declared that 'having shared in the prosperity of their flocks, the clergy of Ireland are willing to share in their privations, and are determined to resist a measure calculated to create vast discontent – to sever the people from their pastors, and ultimately to endanger Catholicity in this country'. To pay the priests was a key strategy for Russell, and although he was no friend of Catholicism and was happy to reduce the influence of the priests, his motivation was a desire to improve the status of the church of the majority and relieve the poor of a heavy burden. Faced with the opposition of the Catholic bishops, on the one hand, and of the many Protestants on the other, he abandoned, what was a central plank in his plan to bring a golden age to Ireland.

Even before Russell's plan for Ireland had unravelled, other events had occurred that made more difficult his attempts to enact remedial measures for Ireland. In the autumn of 1847, a banking crisis had caused alarm and the Treasury became more penny-pinching. That same autumn the elections in England had strengthened the hands of economists who wanted the Irish to fend for themselves, while Ireland returned a record number of members committed to the Repeal of the Union with England, a result Clarendon blamed on the priests. More serious were the repercussions that followed the Mahon murder. Palmerston's memorandum to Minto in Rome, for relaying to the Pope, was explicit: 'the exasperation growing up in the public mind against the Catholic priesthood is extreme and scarcely anybody now talks of these Irish murders without a fervent wish that a dozen priests be hanged forthwith.' He added that 'they are ... the open ... and shameless instigators to violence and murder'. The Young Ireland rebellion deepened the exasperation. Clarendon claimed that the British public had been moved by the suffering in Ireland and had contributed generously, feeling it 'to be a labour of love ... why is all this love turned into bitterness ...? The manner in which it is received, and the attempts to shake off English rule ... The great body of the Catholic clergy promoting all this'. Exasperated, uncomprehending and relief-weary, British public opinion was back on the track of regarding the Irish as incomprehensible, ungrateful, indeed treacherous. They would give no more to rebels and assassins, and their instigators, the Catholic priests.

The priests, on the other hand, already smarting from the

Young Irelanders' criticisms that they counselled calm to a perishing people, were outraged at being slandered to the world, and especially to the Pope, as instigators of assassination. It was an English plot, they believed, to discredit the church and leave it at the mercy of a hostile state. As the distress worsened again, a conviction gradually emerged, which later became more widely held, that, in Ireland, the government was failing to relieve the people effectively and to fulfil its primary duty of saving life. Recrimination and counter-recrimination had brought old suspicious, national and religious, bubbling to the surface.

CHAPTER 4

Continuing Famine
and Conflicting 'Theologies'

Distress in 1848-50

Despite Trevelyan's authoritative declaration at the end of 1847 that the 'distress', as he euphemistically called the Famine, was over, deaths and distress continued for another four years. When, in the winter of 1848, the potato failed massively again, more frightful suffering resulted, particularly in the west. In 1849, deaths (from all causes) almost equalled those of 1847, as famine, disease and evictions reaped a fearful harvest. As Clarendon told the prime minister, the people were worn out from years of suffering. In April 1848, Fr James Dwyer from Claregalway, acknowledging the gift of £15 from the General Relief Committee, wrote:

> On the evening of the day I received the bountiful contents of your communication, I attended at the sick bed of nine persons in one house, all suffering from typhus ... the father, the mother and seven children – without any means to cool their parched tongues save a drink of cold water and only one feeble female to minister to their pitiful cries in that awful situation. *The nine persons were huddled together in the same room of the cabin!* Oh heavens, what a spectacle! Without anything like covering. I have just learned that death has put an end to the sufferings of the father on yesterday and would in all probability have sim-

ilarly terminated the existence of the others – had not a small trifle from my own scanty resources (they cannot any longer be termed resources) along with the means your bounty supplied me with, enabled me to hand them what, I trust to the mercy of God, may spare the lives of some of them.

On 6 March, 1849, Fr Patrick Quaide, Dromcollogher, Co Limerick, gave a catalogue of suffering that recalled the worst days of Black '47:

> I visited ... Timothy Carroll of Knocktoosh ... one (son) 14 years of age was in bed actually dead, lying by his father and brother's side ... In Carroll's house, there was a family named Daly, six in number ... nine days without relief after having surrendered their land, they were all but dead ... A man passing through Broadford ... fell down and died ... No one would allow the corpse into his house until they opened the chapel where he lay a night in his old rags ... I visited ... Timothy Connors at Boola ... Whilst administering the sacrament to his wife, he was obliged to leave his den of horror and go out on the road. I thought on beholding him, he was one of the savage tribes ... of America. He was literally a skeleton and with the exception of an old coat torn to shreds ... he was literally naked ... He ... was hoarse from roaring with thirst. I procured some drink for him. As I passed next morning, he was relieved of his suffering. His corpse and that of his wife were borne to the grave.

Quaide added that, in one week: 'I attended between two and three hundred sick calls', 'by the ditches, in quarries, in ruined buildings ... in every shape that misery can present itself to view.'

Towards the end of May 1849, Bishop Egan of Kerry, thanking the president of Maynooth College for sending aid, told him of the terrible toll the work houses were taking:

Only those who go among the people can form a correct estimate of their destitution. We have in Killarney five auxiliary workhouses all crammed to such an excess as to contaminate the air and cause every week from 26 to 30 deaths; the mortality is principally amongst the children and the very old persons. You may frequently meet the poor Father who entered the work houses with 4 or 5 children, after a time leaving with one child on his back and assigns as his reason that all the others died and he would rather starve outside than run the risk of losing the only one that as yet survive.

Even people who had some reserves in the first years of the Famine, had now exhausted them. J. H. Lynch, in a plea in *The Tablet* for help for the Carmelite Convent at Knocktopher, affirmed: 'The hands which used to break bread to the hungry are now held out to solicit alms for their own support.' From Cork, the tireless Brother John Leonard reported that the Brothers could no longer continue the meal a day for the 300 children and had to reduce the number to 90 'who being fatherless or orphans could not possibly be abandoned. Such is the deplorable state of things here, that they have now increased to 140 for whom no means of relief but the occasional offering of the charitable.'

Evictions and exposure added to the suffering, as Fr Ward of Partry, told Bishop Briggs:

Upwards of 1700 individuals fell victim in this remote and mountainous parish to this devouring famine. More than 700 houses are levelled to the ground by cruel landlords, and their inmates wandering with scarcely a rag to cover their nakedness, shivering with cold, worn by the agonies of fever and exposed to the piercing blasts of winter. My Lord, did the good and humane people of England know of our ... woeful condition they would not fail to pity us.

As Ward implied, if the distress had been more 'visible', if it had occurred in England, government and public opinion might have been more generous in their response.

Fr Peter Ward of Ballinrobe related in March 1849 that 'nearly 800 houses are already levelled to the ground by our cruel landlords. The poor seeking shelter in dikes and ditches and dying in numbers.' In January, Fr Matthew McQuaid of Killeshandra wrote to *The Freeman's Journal*, 'There never was perhaps a more terrible persecution against the poor than at the present moment. There seems to be a hellish rivalry among some agents as to who will banish the most.'

Evictions reached the record number of 13,384 families in 1849 and, perhaps it is not surprising that in October two Catholic priests, Fr Thomas O'Shea and Matthew O'Keefe, founded, in Callan, County Kilkenny, the first successful Tenant Right movement. Before long a number of Presbyterian ministers joined it.

The Poor Law Extension Act of 1847 had permitted some re-lief to be given outside the work houses, usually at the gate. The conditions for this 'outdoor relief' were so stringent, however, that it was proving hopelessly inadequate, as Fr O'Reilly of Bangor Erris recounted:

> the outdoor relief is ... an empty name – to our able-bodied poor it is denied until brought to the last degree of exhaus-tion; and even if then admitted, the quantity is generally not more than half that allowed by law. Our distance from the work houses is another of our grievances, this parish being in part about 26 miles from it, and yet notwithstand-ing the distance, some unfortunate fathers and mothers, each carrying a child or two, had in the depth of winter to attend three reviews lest they should be too heavy in flesh for outdoor relief and it not unfrequently happened that some, after being rejected as not qualified for relief, have been found dead along the ditches in their attempt to reach their homes.

Fr Timblin, parish priest of Kill, Ballina, related how hundreds of his parishioners had been struck off the relief lists so that now 'we are between the dying and the dead every hour of the day … the awful wretched condition of the great majority of the people of Tyrawly is far beyond description'.

Archbishop Murray and others were still sending relief money and the need was never greater. Peter Ward, parish priest of Ballinrobe, describes the scene when relief arrived in March 1849. 'I had been in chapel surrounded by several hundreds of my poor parishioners praying for our benefactors, when your happy letter arrived. It is hard to describe their sensation as well as mine on the occasion. They and I were without one single penny.' When Bishop Fennelly sent £15.10.6 from Madras to *The Tablet* fund, no less than nine priests from different parts of the country were immediately scrambling for a share for their parishioners. *The Tablet* fund also received £10 from the professor of Irish at Maynooth, Fr Tully, and £5 apiece from his two colleagues, Fr Thomas Farrelly, the college bursar and Dr Callan, the scientist, three regular contributors of relief. Private charity became more crucial in 1849 but, as the Society of Friends pointed out, only government intervention could cope with the scale of the catastrophe and this was not forthcoming.

'Fireworks in Glasnevin'

Queen Victoria had given, not the traditional derisory £5 for famine relief but £2,000 and had led a national day of prayer and atonement on 24 March 1847. Now, in 1849, Clarendon, the viceroy, and the prime minister, hoped that a visit by her might boost morale and be a symbol and celebration of the unity of all subjects in the United Kingdom. It was agreed that she should come on 3 August. A year earlier, when 20,000 of the leading people in Ireland signed an address thanking the Queen for her efforts for relief, it was noted that, although almost all the clergy of the Established Church signed it, few Catholic bishops had done so. Would the Catholic clergy now welcome her? The three archbishops

(Archbishop Crolly of Armagh had died of cholera) had sharply different reactions to the news of the visit. Archbishop Murray, who normally wrote the hierarchy's addresses, circulated a draft address of warm welcome. MacHale of Tuam, angrily rejected it:

> I could not affix my signature to any form of address deficient in the expression of those evangelical duties to our flocks, suffering from famine and cruelty, on which Christian bishops should not be silent ... I regret I find no allusion whatever to the sufferings of the people, or the causes under the control of legislative enactment by which their sufferings are still aggravated.

MacHale drew up an alternative text which underscored the appalling mortality that 'has in several parts of Ireland, diminished your Majesty's subjects by a fourth, and in some by a half', the 'cruel evictions' and the suffering from Famine. Even when Murray inserted a reference in the address to 'the many woes of our suffering poor', MacHale complained that 'it leaves the original address still liable to the same objections of being entirely silent on the hideous cruelty inflicted, for want of legislative government protection, on our flocks whom we see daily, through the operations of those very cruelties, perishing unpitied before our eyes.' Archbishop Slattery of Cashel, too, demanded that the desolation caused by Famine be spelt out and rejected Murray's draft as 'a milk and water address'. Both he and MacHale refused to sign the address, or to accept the invitation to the Queen's levee. Murray could persuade only twelve bishops to sign the address.

Other prominent clergy too, were critical. Appalled at costly celebrations amid such suffering, Fr John Miley, Daniel O'Connell's companion on his last journey to Rome, told Fr Spratt that the celebrations in Dublin were 'like illuminating a graveyard – like fireworks in Glasnevin, or like shutting out, with a gorgeous curtain, one half of a long ward of an hospital crowded with all kinds of disease and suffering'.

Limerick clergy drew up their own address to the Queen: 'Madam,' they wrote, 'in no other region of the habitable globe would it be permitted to two or three satraps ... to un-roof and demolish at their pleasure the homes of fifteen thou-sand human beings, and to turn out that multitude ... to die by the slow wasting of famine and disease.' This reaction to the Royal Visit is significant. The mood of the clergy had changed since autumn 1846. Then they trusted in govern-ment action. Now they were angry at the government for its inadequate response to the Famine and angry, too, at any cover-up of the suffering of the Famine victims. That feeling was shortly to find a more public expression.

Poverty, Providence and the Synod of Thurles 1850

No bishops' meeting was held in 1849 for it was decided to hold a National Synod in 1850, the first since the seventeenth century. The Synod was to deal with the issue of the Queen's Colleges, which was still dividing the hirearchy, and matters of discipline. It was presided over by Paul Cullen, who had lately arrived from Rome as Archbishop of Armagh and Papal Legate, and it was held at Thurles, from 22 August to 10 September. At the conclusion of this important Synod, which marks the coming of age of the modern Irish church, the bishops issued an 'Address to the Catholic clergy and laity'. It was a wide-ranging document and took a stand on the problems facing the country. It provides a valuable in-sight into the bishops' attitude to Famine-related questions.

Mindful of the constant accusations that clergy were inciting the people to violence, the bishops first carefully but categori-cally claimed it as their right and duty, enjoined on them at their ordination, to defend the poor. The decrees of every general council, from Chalcedon in the fifth century to Trent in the sixteenth, express 'concern for the poor' and so they, the bishops, would be guilty of 'criminal neglect if they suffer the poor to be oppressed without raising their voice in their defence and vindication.' While exhorting the poor to respect the rights of property and the social order, they made a vigorous protest on their behalf:

> We behold our poor not only crushed and overwhelmed by the awful visitation of heaven, but frequently the victims of the most ruthless oppression that ever disgraced the annals of humanity. Though they have been made to the image of the living God, and are purchased by the blood of Calvary, though the special favourites and representatives of Jesus Christ, we see them treated with a cruelty that would cause the heart to ache if inflicted on the beasts of the field ...

Then in a breathtaking description of the effects of the evictions the Address went on:

> the desolating track of the Exterminator is to be traced in too many parts of the country – in those levelled cottages and roofless abodes where so many virtuous and industrious families have been torn by brute force, without distinction of age or sex, sickness or health, and flung upon the highway to perish in the extremity of want.

Whereas the blight was a 'visitation of heaven', the evictions were 'ruthless oppression'. Solemnly warning those evictors that the arm of the Lord was not shortened, the Address quoted the Letter of St James that 'the hire of the labourers, who have reaped down your fields, which by fraud has been kept back by you, crieth, and the cry of them has entered into the ears of the Lord of Sabaoth'. After thus threatening 'the exterminators' with the vengeance of God, the bishops then launched an attack on the prevailing economico-philosophical attitude of the day and its attitude to the poor, which they identified as the root cause of such heartless actions:

> One of the worst fruits of the false teaching of the age, has been to generate a spirit of contempt, hard heartedness, and hostility to the poor. The Mammon of iniquity, not the Spirit of Christianity, and ... avarice ..., not the charity of

Jesus Christ, have furnished the principles and maxims by which they have been estimated and ranked in the social scale. While the Gospel everywhere breathes respect, love, and commiseration for the destitute ... the spirit of error, on the contrary ... denounces them as the great nuisance of the moral world ...

The bishops, after their meetings, normally presented their address or memorial to the viceroy. This time they addressed the entire Catholic people – clerics and laity. It was also significant in that, in addition to castigating the 'extermination' – now their normal term for evictions – they focused on the ideology that made such treatment of the poor acceptable.

When the government learned of the Address, its fury was unbounded. Clarendon had hoped that the Synod would not condemn the Queen's Colleges, but not only had the bishops rejected the Colleges scheme but they had, unexpectedly, raised the whole issue of the treatment of the poor, promoting, as he saw it, 'the disruption of all social ties'. Angrily he denounced the 'mummers of Thurles', as he called the bishops, for setting the poor against the rich, and branded their Address as 'worthy of Louis Blanc for its socialist doctrines'. He pointed out, too, that in the Address, 'no remark is made upon the conduct ... of that portion of the clergy which endeavoured to throw the country into rebellion and to produce in Ireland that anarchy ... which has prevailed throughout Europe and which here as elsewhere would have established infidelity upon the ruins of society.' It was high time, he said, to inquire whether 'we shall permit a set of men under the mask of religion ... to preach a crusade against civilisation and to stir up different classes against each other'. His threat appeared to take on substance when, a few months later, parliament passed the 'Ecclesiastical Titles' Bill which condemned the pastoral letter in which Cardinal Wiseman announced the setting up of a Catholic hierarchy in England as 'papal aggression'. In introducing this bill, the last penal leg-

islation against the Catholic church passed by a British parliament, the prime minister shifted the blame from Wiseman's
pastoral to the Irish bishops' Address, alleging that in it 'no
language was omitted which could excite the feelings of the
peasant class against those who were owners of the land.'

1849-50: Government Inaction

Despite the government's fury at the bishops for pronouncing
so forcibly on social issues in the manner they did in the
Address, the appalling state of the country warranted some
comment. Not only had the deaths in 1849 approached the
record level of 1847, but evictions had soared to 90,000 and
reached 104,000 in 1850; emigration had reached the highest
level yet. Worse still, Russell no longer had any plan to deal
with the catastrophe. In his diary for 9 February 1849, that
acute observer, Charles Greville, the secretary to the cabinet,
noted with horror the confusion, paralysis and hard-heartedness within the cabinet. The people in Ireland were dying of
hunger, he recorded, and no one knew what to do. 'All call on
the government for a plan and a remedy, but the government
have no plan and no remedy; there is nothing but disagree-
ment among them; and while they are discussing and disput-
ing, the masses are dying ... Charles Wood (the Chancellor of
the Exchequer) has all along set his face against giving or
lending money ... and he contemplates ... that all the misery
and distress should run their course.' The commercial crisis
in 1847 had reinforced the reaction against relief and enabled
Wood and Trevelyan to make economy the order of the day.
Officials in Dublin, however, closer to the famine scene, were
alarmed at the scale of distress and Clarendon, the viceroy,
totally converted to the need for government aid, complained bitterly: 'I have ... expressed my fears that the doctrines of Trevelyan, whose mouthpiece C. Wood is, would
prevail ... C. Wood, backed by Grey (another cabinet minister), and relying upon arguments (or rather Trevelyanisms)
that are no more applicable to Ireland than to Loo Choo, af-

firmed that the right thing to do was to do nothing – they have prevailed and you see what a fix we are in.' Pleading with the prime minister for aid, Clarendon savagely attacked the attitude of those ministers: 'Wood and Trevelyan,' he alleged, 'sat cooly watching and applauding what they call "the operation of natural causes."' While Wood, anxious to reduce government expenditure, told Russell: 'I am perfectly ready to give them (the Irish) as near nothing as may be', other cabinet ministers, Lords Clanricarde and Landsdowne, Irish landlords themselves, strove to limit the amount landlords would have to pay to support the poor. It was all too much for Edward Twistleton, the chief commissioner of the Poor Laws in Ireland, who, after clashes with the Treasury, finally resigned, claiming that the indifference of the British parliament was leading to 'a policy of extermination'.

The ineffectual Russell was not in control of his cabinet and he saw his dream for Ireland vanish. Yet in a remarkable admission to Clarendon, he gave his own view of the problem: 'the great difficulty ... respecting Ireland,' he maintained, 'is one which does not spring from Trevelyan or C. Wood but lies deep in the breasts of the British people. It is this – we have granted, lent, subscribed, worked, visited, clothed the Irish, millions of money, years of debate ... the only return is calumny and rebellion – let us not grant, clothe ... any more and see what that will do.' The cabinet merely reflected British public opinion as expressed by the press, parliament and people and it was one of national misunderstanding, exasperation and, indeed, hostility, towards the Irish.

'The Hand of Providence'?

The bishops in their defence of the poor, had also identified an underlying attitude, that was not directly connected with national antagonism but had its source in both economic and religious thought. Classical economics, to which Routh and Russell had referred Irish delegations seeking aid, opposed interference with economic development and market forces, even if that entailed suffering for the poor. Furthermore, since society was religious in outlook, both British and Irish people accepted that the hand of God was discernible in natural catastrophes. Many further believed that such catastrophes occurred for a specific and providential purpose. Trevelyan, an Evangelical Protestant, whose influence on relief was paramount, believed that the Famine was 'the judgement of God on an indolent and unself-reliant people'. As God had 'sent the calamity to teach the Irish a lesson, that calamity must not be too much mitigated'. Since the Famine was God's providential way of teaching the indolent Irish to change their ways, the hard-working English nation should not alleviate it too much. It was 'the cure ... applied by the direct stroke of an all wise providence in a manner as unexpected ... as it is likely to be effectual'! Trevelyan believed that the famine might prove the providential occasion to change Irish behaviour and society for good. Many influential people thought like him.

'Providence' was a common category for Christians to invoke in explanation of natural catastrophes and the Irish clergy, too, had invoked it earlier in the famine, as when Fr Mathew lamented to Trevelyan that 'Divine providence has again poured out upon us the vial of its wrath' or Murray wrote: 'We are not yet independent of providence'. The Synod of Thurles itself spoke of the 'awful visitation of heaven'. Their view of providence, however, was more a recognising and acceptance that providence, for some mysterious design, permitted suffering and evil, a variant on the prayer common in rural Ireland: 'Welcome be the will of God.' At the same time, all their statements insisted strongly on the duty of the rich to help the poor. Pope Pius IX, in his encyclical on the Famine, *Praedecessores Nostros*, does not use the word 'providence' or its equivalent, but speaks of 'beseeching God, the father of mercies, to free the Irish people from this great disaster', while he implores the faithful to 'vigorously assist the poor'.

Some angrier voices questioned a facile evoking of providence as the cause of the catastrophe. The Cavan-born Bishop Hughes of New York had solemnly warned: 'Let us be careful not to blaspheme providence by calling this God's famine.'. Priests, eyewitnesses of the misery, also rejected that 'providential' interpretation. Already in 1846, Fr Mullins of Clarenbridge, County Galway, angrily protesting the death, in six months, of 75 of his parishioners – 55 of them from starvation – exclaimed agonisingly: 'How is all this desolation to be accounted for? Surely it was not caused by the visitation of an angry providence, but by the crying injustice of our earthly rulers'! In 1848, Fr Nicholas Coughlan, complaining of 'the unworthy death of some 800,000 honest men' declared emphatically: 'as to this heavy scourge coming from holy providence, I believe none of it; I rather believe it comes *from beyond the (Irish) channel* ...' While these angry statements may appear to discard the very notion of providence in the face of so enormous a human catastrophe, the context in which they are written indicates rather a rejection of the indiscriminate invocation of providence to cloak human responsibility. As evictions increased and their horror revealed the hand of man rather than the hand of God, by 1849, the clergy, eye-witnesses of the scenes, were horrified at the failure to protect the poor from what the Synod described as 'the most ruthless oppression that ever disgraced the annals of humanity'. Others thought the same. In horrified terms, William Bennett of the Society of Friends reported: 'they are dying like cattle off the face of the earth, from want and its kindred horrors. Is this to be regarded in the light of a Divine dispensation and punishment?' A contemporary poet, Máire Ní Dhroma, from Rinn, Co Waterford, wrote:

> Ní hé Dia 'cheap riamh an obair seo,
> Daoine bochta a chur le fuacht is le fán
> (It was never God who thought up this work,
> Of casting out poor people to wander in the cold.)

The bishops' Thurles Address can be seen as an attempt to counter the ideology of Trevelyan and of the political economists. It was on the question of culpability and the attitude to the poor that they pointed to the sharpest differences. They had already, in their memorial to the viceroy in 1847, rejected any attempt to blame the famine on 'the indolence of the peasants', laying it instead on the 'penal laws' which had deprived people of both property rights and the fruits of their labour. Now again, in the Address, they insisted that those 'flung upon the highway to perish' were not indolent, but 'virtuous and industrious families'. Behind that failure to halt evictions and protect life, they discerned an attitude which they considered alien to the Gospel – a contempt for the poor whom many of the governing class saw as a drag on the progress of the United Kingdom and 'the great nuisance of the moral world ...' The bishops reminded Christians that the poor 'were made to the image of the living God and are purchased by the blood of Calvary' and 'the special favourites and representatives of Jesus Christ'. Earlier on Fr Spratt, the founder of two relief organisations, demanded more food of the government officials for their starving fellow creatures, who were created by the same omnipotent God, and were as much entitled to live as themselves, and Fr Edward Waldron insisted that the poor, too, were 'made to God's image and likeness' and should be so treated. The contact with the poor, who formed a majority of their faithful, made clergy sensitive to their plight. It is arguable, too, that the bishops and clergy represented an older, more accepting attitude to the poor, whereas the attitude becoming prevalent in Britain reflected, in part, a more modern post-industrial revolution attitude and a different work-ethic.

Evangelical Missions

'Providence' as interpreted by some Evangelical Protestants, was the cause of another concern that agitated the Catholic clergy in the latter years of the Famine. Many Evangelicals saw the Famine as the opportunity provided by providence for the conversion of Catholics. In the enthusiastic words of one of them, the Reverend C. Richards, 'There was never such a time as the present open in Ireland ... for the preaching ... of the light of the ... Gospel'.

Most great religions feel morally bound to propagate their message of salvation, by making converts or proselytes. Yet what one religious group regards as missionary activity, the opposing group perceives as immoral poaching; when a religious body believes that outside its church there is no salvation, enticing a person to leave it is perceived as little short of demonic. Inextricably intertwined with the spiritual dimension, are other dimensions – social, cultural and political.

All these elements were present in nineteenth century Ireland for, despite warm co-operation between religious bodies on Famine relief, this was not an ecumenical age. Since the 1820s, Evangelical Protestants had launched a zealous campaign, often referred to as the 'Second Reformation', to convert Catholics. During the Famine, they redoubled their efforts. Their efforts became more organised when, in 1849, Alexander Dallas founded the Society for Irish Church Missions to Roman Catholics, with headquarters in London and branches throughout the United Kingdom. By 1854, it had set up 125 mission stations in Ireland, an indication of the zeal of the missionaries and the generosity of their supporters. Their main motivation was to rescue the people from the darkness of popery and to bring them the pure light of the gospel which, in turn, would render them peaceful and more open to political integration.

Of critical importance in any missionary activity is the means it adopts or is perceived to adopt. There were numerous complaints that some evangelicals used food, clothing, and other material benefits to win converts. Already in 1847, the delegation of the Catholic bishops, led by Archbishops Murray and Crolly, in their respectful memorial to Clarendon, the viceroy, had protested against 'the unchristian abuse of public and private charities evinced by the wicked attempts at proselytism'. When he failed to address their problem, they immediately renewed their protest. A few years later Clarendon, who disliked Catholicism, himself expressed concern. When the Duke of Bedford, the prime minister's brother, told Clarendon that the Mission Society had formed a branch in Bedford, the viceroy commented apprehensively that, 'A Protestant movement is going on in the Diocese of Tuam, and I hope some of the conversions may be sincere and lasting, but one cannot feel sure when food and clothing are brought in aid of the Scriptures. If a branch is established at Bedford I suppose you can hardly avoid subscribing to it. As Lord Lieutenant I should not venture to do so as its objects are proselytising and *if* it effects some good, it is at the cost of much bad blood.'

Bad blood was unfortunately created. Later, the Quaker, Alfred Webb, noted perceptively in his diary:

> A network of well-intentioned Protestant associations spread over the poorer parts of the country, which in return for soup and other help endeavoured to gather the people into their churches and schools, really believing that masses of our people wished to abandon Catholicism … The movement left seeds of bitterness.'

Clarendon and Webb were correct as regards 'seeds of bitterness'. Catholics were convinced then and later that the Evangelicals made use of soup, food, clothing and money to persuade the starving poor to attend their services, a practice that Catholics labelled 'taking the soup' or 'souperism'.

A full assessment of this complex and sensitive question falls outside the scope of this volume which is principally concerned with the perception and experience of the Catholic clergy as it emerges from their correspondence. This correspondence reveals that, although anxiety existed from the beginning of the Famine, it increased during its closing years to become a main topic in the bishop's letters in the early 1850s. From the beginning of the Famine, clergy in Cork, Kerry, Limerick, Mayo, Sligo and Dublin had complained increasingly about aggressive proselytism. In 1847, Michael Enright, parish priest of Castletown Beare, reported that 'a whole bevy of parsons is to be seen every hour of the day going from house to house distributing tracts and pouring the vilest calumnies on our religion'. The effectiveness of these efforts varied, he added. 'Indignation is excited in the minds of the great number. Others begin for the first time to entertain doubts of their religion and a few are seduced or prevailed on to act as if they had changed their religious opinions.' Reverend Edward Nangle had been an active Evangelical missioner in Achill for many years. Now, in 1848, Michael Gallagher, the parish priest, admitted that 'poverty ... has compelled ... the greater number of the population to send their children to Nangle's proselytising, villainous schools ... They are dying of hunger and rather than die, they have submitted to his impious tenets.' From Clifden, William Flannelly informed Archbishop Murray:

> It cannot be wonder if a starving people be perverted in shoals, especially as they go from cabin to cabin and when they find the inmates naked and starved to death, they proffer food, money and raiment, on the express condition of becoming members of their conventicle ... They are ... saying to the poor people, 'Why not go to your priests and get money from them?'

Martin Harte, parish priest of Ballycastle, in the Killala diocese, complained that the Belfast Societies had bought land to form a colony. 'They have money in abundance and many hearers on Sunday ... They have selected my parish as the most distressed, but (I) hope in God I will be able to banish them as soon as the lumpers (cheaper, but widely-used potato) makes (sic) their appearance.'

Fr Patrick McLoughlin, of Kiltullagh, near Castlereagh, revealed a further complication:

We have here to contend with a Protestant clergyman named Blundell ... The principal landlords are Protestants and bigots, over whom he has a great ascendancy, and uses his influence with them or their agents in removing poor Catholics from their holdings, in order to have them to give to their Protestant neighbours. It is well understood that if they go to church, that they will not be disturbed. He is also well supplied with money, from English charities ... and the use he converts it to is to endeavour to make the poor barter their religion for a little meal or a few stones of seed potatoes.

Then, in an emotional description of many priests predicament, he added:

You cannot imagine what an annoyance such a character must be to poor pennyless priests, who are more than over-worked in running from one end to another of a parish 14 miles in length, badly supplied with roads, at the same time often rising before the sun to prepare to proceed to a distant point of the parish, there to break the bread of life to the Children of the Faith. Our only confidence and safeguard is God's grace and the strong faith of our poor people, who if any should yield, (it) would be at the sacrifice of snapping asunder their hearts' last dearest chords. From such a sad step may the Lord protect them.

Sister Mary O'Donel of the Presentation Convent Galway, claiming that in their zeal the missioners spared no money to bring over the poor, catches the flavour of the Evangelical preaching: '*Money* is to be no obstacle, no sum will be refused to bring over the poor. "Fly from Babylon" is, I believe, the watch word. The priests are called impostors but we (the nuns) are pitied and my darkness is *awful*.'

For the priests, upset and angry at Famine, fever and evictions, this spiritual torment was worse. The cry of agony that went up from some of them sprang from the fact that proselytism was an issue that touched the whole meaning of their life and work. Were they failing in their primary duty of protecting their 'flock', and would they not have to answer to God on the day of judgement? Their anger at the proselytisers was often unmeasured. 'Ill-omened birds of prey', raged Fr Maher of Killeshan. 'Cursed souperism' thundered the very moderate Archdeacon O'Sullivan, who appears to have incited an attack on the local parson, who was beaten 'within an inch of his life'. Cullen was angry at O'Sullivan for his violent action, but, in the privacy of his diary, O'Sullivan defended his conduct, not without some humour:

> Now I am no agitator ... (Yet) if souperism were to invade my parish in the morning, before evening would Fr John (himself) become the greatest agitator in the Country. He would be a Tenant Right man, a Defence Association man, a Repealer, anything, everything, to stir up and excite the people. Prayers and Rosaries and Missions and Forty Hours ... are the only weapons Dr Cullen depends on ... Rome knows very little and Dr Cullen seems to know less of what a priest on a country mission must recur to in order to meet soupers.

The strength of his reaction is an indication of the passions that proselytism aroused. In 1848, in their memorial to the viceroy, the bishops repeated their protest of 1847. In 1850, at the Synod of Thurles, they labelled proselytisers 'Sons of perdition' (*perditos homines*), who sought 'by money, gifts, and all kind of corruption to deprive the starving, afflicted poor of their most precious possession – their faith'. The Synod, however, was careful to point out that the more enlightened of their Protestant brethren were the first to condemn such proselytism.

The co-operation in relief work that had existed between all religions suffered. Relief committees, workhouses, hospitals, asylums and schools all now became religious battlefields. Bad blood was created which obscured the impressive relief

work of the Protestant community not only in Ireland but in
the United States, Britain and throughout the British Empire.

The Exodus

If Clarendon censured proselytism, he took an enthusiastic
view of another phenomenon of Ireland in the 1850s – the
mass emigration. 'Priests and patriots howl over the "Exodus"',
he exulted, 'but the departure of thousands of papist Celts
must be a blessing to the country they quit ... Some English
and Scots settlers have arrived.' Emigration, often regarded
as the solution for getting rid of the surplus population, was
to reach 7, 000 a week in 1852 and *The Times* of London was
forecasting that 'in a few years more a Celtic Irishman will be
as rare in Connemara as is the Red Indian on the shores of
Manhattan'. The clergy grieved to see so many people go, but
as that inveterate nationalist, Fr Maher, declared, he would
rather see his people 'alive in Illinois than rotting in Ireland'.
Archdeacon O'Sullivan told a parliamentary committee that
though he hated with all his soul the loss of the best blood of
Ireland, he had advised 'every man to emigrate because he
believed that every man must place his own life and happi-
ness, and (those) of his dependents before other loyalties'.
'Everyone,' Archbishop Cullen declared in 1851, 'must deplore
the sad circumstances which compel the inhabitants of this
fine country to emigrate from their cherished fatherland' and
he hoped for some means of keeping them at home. Bishop
Moriarty of Kerry commented despondently some years
later: 'The exodus of the people bids fair to solve all questions. They are all going.' The emigration continued unabated.

Although the famine was easing off towards the end of 1851,
there was still much distress. 'I was in Cashel on Tuesday,'
wrote Archbishop Slattery to his friend Laurence Renehan of
Maynooth, 'when I confirmed 1126 inmates of the poorhouses
though in fact the town is but one vast poorhouse. I am not
the better of it yet ... from the appalling spectacle of the place
and the people – in truth my heart sank within me at the sight

– may God help them and us.' In Clare, especially, and in isolated pockets in Munster and Connacht, distress lingered on for another few years.

'Excess of Suffering'

Suffering on such a scale and for so long a period was more than most people could take. At Grosse Île, Father Taschereau experienced how numbed to horrors the victims had become: 'It had always seemed to me that the presence of a dead body in a ship must arouse some kind of feeling, but ... many... have been pointed out to me with a sort of indifference when I passed beside their beds or where we lay them while waiting for the coffins to be ready; I see this as a new mark of degradation caused by an excess of suffering ...' Apart from this numbness, what effect this 'excess of suffering' had on the people is difficult to gauge. Did it bring a sense of shame at what happened, or perhaps a deep-rooted depression and anger at the deaths? There was much heroic sacrifice by family-members, neighbours, doctors, clergymen and relief-workers, but other things had occurred that people wanted to forget. The evictions caused untold suffering. Crimes had multiplied as people strove to survive. Terrible scenes were enacted in work houses and in the indescribable holds of ships, as attendants and victims themselves became inured to the suffering around them. Not all strong farmers had been as generous as the Cullens; some had protected their crops and seed potatoes with shot-gun and trap, while others had taken the farms of the dispossessed. The Famine strengthened the strongest farmers and the graziers, who, with the extinction of the cottiers, were able to extend their holdings.

The famine and the high-level emigration it triggered had important consequences for Irish society and culture and no less for the church. The loss by Famine and emigration of some two and a half million of its faithful could not but produce a profound shock. Certainly, the countryside was forever changed as whole townlands were abandoned. 'Melancholy starvation, heartless extermination and unexampled emigration of our people ... have rendered this poor diocese (in common with the West of Ireland) a wilderness!', Bishop French told Renehan in May 1850. Taken with that loss, the initial, and loudly-trumpeted, success of the Evangelical missions appeared, for a while, to threaten the existence of 'Catholic Ireland'. The resurgence of strident 'no-popery' in Britain sharpened this threat. Parish missions, preached by religious orders, were the means the church used to counter the Evangelicals and to strengthen the Catholic faith of their people. The decline of the Irish language and the growing knowledge of English favoured the spread of a counter-Reformation culture which, up to this, had been confined mainly to towns. These changes might not have come with the same thoroughness had the Famine not devastated the poorer classes, bearers of a more traditional Irish spirituality.

Famine emigrants created 'overseas Irish churches' which provided a distinctive Irish model for the church in all English-speaking lands. These churches were remarkably generous in their support for their kith and kin in Ireland.

Conclusion

The eyewitness accounts of priests and bishops from different parts of Ireland and from abroad, over a period of five or six years, from 1845 to 1851, provide some insight into what the Famine meant for the victims. The cumulative effect of their accounts, so similar in many ways, is to deepen one's realisation of the horror of that terrible experience.

The first reaction of the clergy – total trust in the government – gave way in the autumn of 1846 to disillusion and disbelief. This was followed by despair and hopelessness as, in the early spring of 1847, they looked on helplessly while the Famine swept away whole families, townlands, and villages. They witnessed many of the ties that bound society together come under threat as neighbours were left to lie uncoffined and unburied in the fields and ditches, a prey to wild fowl and animals.

By 1848, evictions and assassinations and the recriminations they generated brought to the surface an anger with the government. Yet, committed to their role of counselling peace, and fearful of the evils rebellion might bring, they had opposed the ill-prepared rebellion of 1848.

When the Famine struck hard again in 1849 and government failed to take any worthwhile measures to relieve the people, this anger grew to find expression in the protest against the Queen's visit, and, in particular, in the increasing militancy of the bishop's recriminations. From 1847 on, they had criticised the inadequacy of relief, the mismanagement in the workhouses, and the misuse of relief funds for proselytism. More significantly, they had rejected the blame for the crisis which the British press and public opinion continued to cast on the peasants. The real problem, they said, was that the subordinate rights of property were given priority over the more fundamental right to life. Then, in their Address from the Synod of Thurles, they went further, fiercely denouncing the evictions taking place under the protection of the law, as no other than the 'track of the Exterminator'. At the root of this 'contempt and hard-heartedness', they identified a perception of the poor as 'a moral nuisance'. To this ideology they opposed a more compassionate one, citing the Gospel as everywhere breathing respect, love, and commiseration for the destitute as the 'special favourites and representatives of Jesus Christ'.

On the practical level, the Catholic church's worldwide relief work was a striking achievement and it reflects credit on its members, lay and clerical, Irish and foreign. On the spiritual level the priests, at deadly risk to themselves, brought the victims, in the words of Bernard O'Reilly, 'the supreme consolation of an Irish Catholic – the last rites of his church.'

Further Reading

The following list is a brief selection.

Thomas P. O'Neill, 'The Catholic Clergy and the Great Famine', *Reportorium Novum* i. (1956), 461-9; a general survey by an expert on Famine relief.

M. Coen, 'Gleanings – The Famine in Galway,' *Connaught Tribune*, March, April, May 1975. An interesting series of articles based on extensive original research.

David C. Sheehy, 'Archbishop Murray of Dublin and the Great Famine in Mayo', *Cathair na Mart*, 11 (1991) 118-28; 'Archbishop Daniel Murray of Dublin and the response of the Catholic Church to the Great Famine in Ireland', *Linkup*, December 1995, pp. 38-42; two lectures by the archivist of the Dublin Diocesan Archives based on his unrivalled knowledge of the papers of Dr Murray.

Peter Grey, 'The triumph of dogma: ideology and Famine relief', *History Ireland* (Summer 1965) pp. 26-34.

Kevin Whelan, 'Tionchar an Ghorta', Cathal Poirtéir (ed.) *Gnéithe den Ghorta* (Coiscéim, Dublin, 1995), pp 41-54.

John Cussen, 'Notes on Famine Times in Newcastle West', *Journal of the Newcastle West Historical Society*, ii (1996), 25-7.

Cormac Ó Gráda, *An Drochshaol: Béaloideas agus Amhráin* (Coiscéim, Dublin, 1994).

Donal A. Kerr, 'A Nation of Beggars?' *Priests, People, and Politics in Famine Ireland 1846-1852* (Oxford University Press, 1995); Donal A. Kerr, *Peel, Priests, and Politics: Sir Robert Peel's Administration and the Roman Catholic Church in Ireland 1841-*

1846 (Oxford University Press, 1982). These two volumes contain sources for citations in the present work.

On the Church of Ireland and the Famine, *Church of Ireland Gazette*, Aug – Sept 1995.

The Christian Brothers' History of the Institute, 3 vols (Dublin, 1958-61).

On Grosse Île: Marianna O'Gallagher and Rose Masson Dompierre, *Eyewitness, Grosse Îsle*, 1847 (Carraig Books, Sainte-Foy, Quebec, 1995), an invaluable collection of letters and documents, together with commentary and biographical detail, from which the extracts cited above are taken.

Pádraig Breandán Ó Laighin, 'Samhradh an Bhróin: Grosse Île, 1847', Cathal Poirtéir (ed) *Gnéithe den Ghorta* (Dublin, 1995), pp 192-231: an important re-appraisal of events at Gross Île.

On Saint Patrick's Day 1996, Sheila Copps, Canadian deputy prime minister and minister of Canadian Heritage, announced that 'in recognition of the importance of Grosse Île, and to mark the upcoming 150th anniversary of the island's greatest tragedy and greatest display of human decency, I am honoured to announce that this … site will be known as "Grosse-Île and the Irish Memorial".' Under the direction of Dr André Charbonneau, due recognition will be given to the fate of the many thousand Irish emigrants who, as the French inscription on the Celtic Cross on the island declares, 'to preserve the faith, suffered hunger and exile … and victims of typhus, finished here their sorrowful pilgrimage, consoled and fortified by the Canadian priest.'

Index of places and key people